Christianity: A Very Short Introduction

VERY SHORT INTRODUCTIONS are for anyone wanting a stimulating and accessible way in to a new subject. They are written by experts, and have been translated into more than 40 different languages.

The Series began in 1995, and now covers a wide variety of topics in every discipline. The VSI library now contains over 350 volumes—a Very Short Introduction to everything from Psychology and Philosophy of Science to American History and Relativity—and continues to grow in every subject area.

Very Short Introductions available now:

Available soon:

For more information visit our website

www.oup.com/vsi/

Linda Woodhead

CHRISTIANITY

A Very Short Introduction

SECOND EDITION

OXFORD
UNIVERSITY PRESS

OXFORD
UNIVERSITY PRESS

Great Clarendon Street, Oxford, OX2 6DP,
United Kingdom

Oxford University Press is a department of the University of Oxford.
It furthers the University's objective of excellence in research, scholarship,
and education by publishing worldwide. Oxford is a registered trade mark of
Oxford University Press in the UK and in certain other countries

First published 2004
Second edition published 2014

Published in the United States of America by Oxford University Press
198 Madison Avenue, New York, NY 10016, United States of America

British Library Cataloguing in Publication Data
Data available

Library of Congress Control Number: 2014937967

ISBN 978-0-19-968774-9

Printed and bound by
CPI Group (UK) Ltd, Croydon, CR0 4YY

Contents

List of illustrations

Introduction

Christianity is one of the world's most successful religions. It has endured over two thousand years and, despite various setbacks, has enjoyed its greatest growth and spread in the modern period.

Part of its success lies in its variety and adaptability. Christianity has a vast reservoir of resources for shaping life and death. Like most religions, it is more capacious and flexible than a philosophical system, and works not only with abstract concepts but with vivid narratives, resonant symbols, living communities, and life-shaping rituals. It appeals to the heart and the senses as well as the mind, and it offers a range of prompts and provocations to guide and shape the lives of individuals and groups. There are nevertheless limits to what can count as Christian, for in opening up some possibilities for human existence it rules out others.

The first two chapters of this book introduce the basic Christian repertoire. They set out some key themes of Christian life and thought, and indicate the foundational resources with which Christians work. Since Christianity is shaped around a man, Jesus Christ, the first chapter outlines the range of ways in which he has been interpreted, and the role these understandings play in setting the boundaries of Christian thought and possibility. The second chapter continues this introductory work, hovering high over

Christianity in order to pick out the signs, stories, symbols, and rituals that serve as the basic building blocks of the religion.

The picture which emerges is of a faith with its origins in an explosion of spiritual energy. This energy—focused and channelled by Jesus Christ—empowered his followers to think, feel, and desire in new ways. In the first centuries of Christian history it gave rise to a wide range of different spiritual movements and to many different versions of the faith. The remainder of the book sketches the growth and spread of the religion across the globe over more than two thousand years, delves deeper into its main varieties, and explains how Christianity has developed in the modern period, documenting both its development into a truly global religion, and its difficult relationship with various aspects of modernity.

Since writing the first edition of this book in 2004, Christianity has changed a great deal. My ideas about it have also moved on, influenced by research I have carried out in various parts of the world, and by the work of other scholars. I have revised and reorganized the entire volume to take account of this, and have added a significant amount of new material. But the underlying approach of the original book remains. Three main types of Christianity are distinguished in terms of how they understand and embody authority and power, both human and divine, and how this plays out in their own structures and their stances towards wider society. I call these the Church, mystical, and biblical types of Christianity. They offer a key to unlock the complexity of the religion's development across time and territory.

This little book draws on a lifetime spent studying and living with different kinds of Christianity, both Catholic and Protestant. It reflects my training in theology, religious studies, history, and sociology. By temperament I am hostile to idealization and attracted to realism. The aim of the book is not to pass judgement on Christianity but to present as well-informed and honest a portrait as I can.

Chapter 1
Jesus: the God-man

The figure of Jesus Christ is both a focus of unity for Christianity and a cause of division. Whatever else they might disagree about, Christians are united in their belief that Jesus Christ has unique significance. Yet they differ over how to explain it. Despite strenuous attempts in all ages to contain Jesus within a single interpretative framework, he repeatedly breaks free.

This ability to escape categorization goes back to Jesus himself. When he spoke he used riddles and parables which even his contemporaries had a hard time understanding. When he referred to himself he used ambiguous titles like 'son of man', or turned the question 'who do you say I am?' back to his questioners. He laid down few clear rules, left no systematic teaching, and founded no institution to pass on his message. Rather than supplying answers he provokes people to make their own response.

Jesus' elusiveness is also a function of the sources on which we rely. We cannot consult the books he wrote because there are none—he may well have been illiterate. We cannot read the words his scribes recorded—he had no scribes. We cannot turn to contemporary accounts of his life and works—there are no accounts. Where Jesus is concerned we have only interpretations and interpretations of interpretations. Even the most important sources of information are already embroiled in the debate about who he was—they already take sides.

And where Jesus is concerned, the boundaries of interpretation could not be broader. It is hard enough to give a reliable account of the life of any individual—biographers make a living out of the fact that there can never be a single, definitive interpretation. But where Jesus is concerned the difficulty is multiplied, for the issue is not simply 'what sort of a man are we dealing with?' but 'are we dealing with man or God?'.

The gospel truth

The search for Jesus begins with the brief documents on which our knowledge rests: the gospels. A gospel is a genre of literature unique to early Christianity. Its name speaks its aim, for the old English word 'gospel' is a translation of the Greek *euangelion* meaning 'good news'. Prior to Christianity, the word was chiefly used in relation to political propaganda about the Roman emperors. To the extent that they aim to propagate an exalted view of the person they describe, the gospels are also propaganda. What they tell us is that Jesus was more than an emperor, more than a prophet, more than any mere mortal. The way you respond to them will seal your fate. No neutral stance is possible in relation to a gospel. Either you believe what it says about Jesus or you do not. Either it will turn out to be good news for you or bad.

Not all gospels convey the same information about Jesus. This is apparent even in the four gospels of Matthew, Mark, Luke, and John, which are included in the New Testament. The latter is the shorter second half of the Bible, composed of around 27 short books written in Greek at various points in the first two centuries of the Christian era (CE or AD—*anno domini* 'year of the Lord'). These four gospels were considered early and authoritative enough to be included. Nevertheless, they differ from one another at many points. Read them in parallel, and you will soon notice differences in both fact and interpretation. Many of the differences are significant: not all the gospels offer an account of Jesus' birth, for example, and Mark's gospel has no stories about the risen Jesus.

The differences are even greater when you take into account the gospels that were not included in the Bible. The Bible joins together the New Testament with the Old Testament, the latter consisting of the scriptures of the Jewish people written in Hebrew, but appropriated by Christians in a later Greek version. The content of the Bible was largely agreed upon by Christian leaders in the latter part of the 4th century AD, though there were—and still are—disagreements between different varieties of Christianity concerning the inclusion of a handful of books. Christians consider the books included in their Bibles authoritative and 'canonical', whereas books which are not included are called 'non-canonical' or 'apocryphal'.

Many apocryphal gospels were destroyed or lost, but some survive either whole or in parts—such as the Gospel of Thomas and the Gospel of Peter (some have been rediscovered only quite recently). Some apocryphal gospels have overlaps with the canonical gospels of Matthew, Mark, Luke, and John, but most offer alternative portrayals and sayings of Jesus.

The inconsistency between the many different gospels can be explained by their varied origins and purpose. Before theology came into being, gospels were one of the chief means by which individuals and groups propagated their distinctive understandings of Jesus and his significance. Most Christian groups probably had access only to a single gospel, and it was much later that a complete New Testament, let alone a complete Bible, became available—and then only to the very wealthy. Different gospels reflect the interests, beliefs, concerns, and rivalries of the many groups that made up what is misleadingly referred to as *the* early church. In fact there were many churches and many gospels (Figure 1). Despite attempts to impose unity,

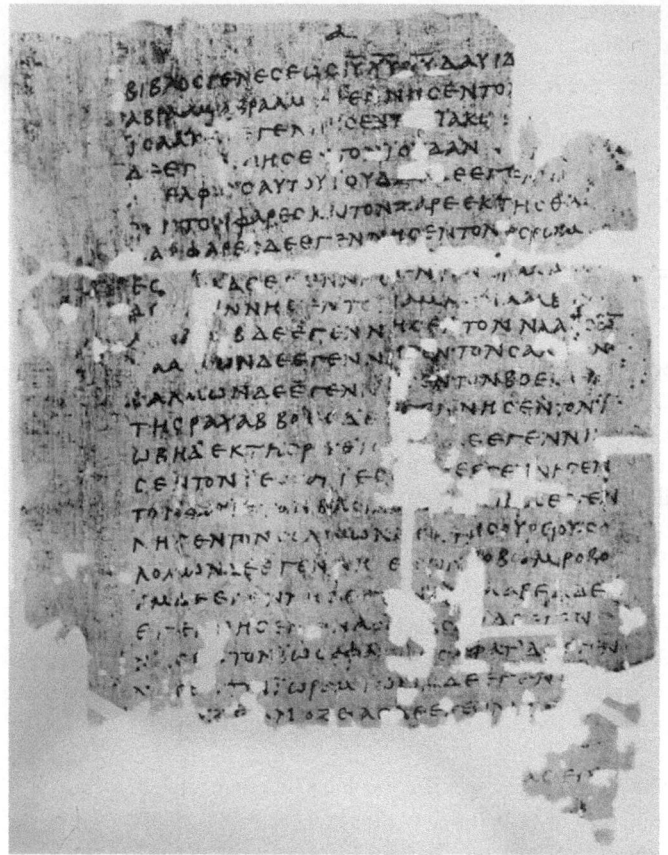

1. An early Christian codex

enough survives to make it clear that Jesus has always meant different things to different people.

The biblical Jesus

Later chapters explain the long historical process whereby one version of Christianity came to establish itself as *the* authoritative, 'orthodox', and 'catholic' (universal) form. What is important at this point is to appreciate that it was this version which laid down the authorized account of Jesus which has shaped the Christian imagination ever since. For now we can put to one side questions of its historical truth, because the canonical Jesus is far more influential than any 'real' Jesus who lies behind the gospels and inspires their portraits. So far as history is concerned, it is the Jesus of the New Testament who has inspired more lives and worked more miracles than the elusive figure historians struggle to reconstruct.

Although the canonical gospels tell us about selected events in Jesus' life, they are not biographies in anything like the modern sense. Only Matthew and Luke give us brief glimpses of Jesus' infancy. Put together, they tell stories of a virgin birth, Mary and Joseph's journey into Egypt, wise men and shepherds paying homage to the baby Jesus born in a stable, and the miraculous learning displayed by the young man. The intention of these preambles is to establish Jesus' unique status, not to probe his formative years and developing psyche.

The gospels' main narrative begins at the point when Jesus' public ministry starts, when he is already mature, perhaps in his late twenties or early thirties. They offer a story of two halves, the first dealing with Jesus' itinerant ministry in his native region of Galilee, and the second with his death in Jerusalem and the events surrounding it. The hinge is the journey he takes from Galilee in the north to Jerusalem in Judea in the south (both parts of ancient Israel and home to the Jewish people, and in Jesus' day under the control of the Roman Empire).

The first half of the narrative establishes Jesus as a teacher and miracle worker. Though baptized by John the Baptist, he launches out on his own and wins followers. Jesus works almost exclusively amongst his own people, the Jews, and acknowledges their God and scriptures. He offers an interpretation of the Jewish faith that is critical of the religious elite and favourable to those who are poor, humble, and socially despised.

The second part of the story is set in Jerusalem, where Jesus' provocative ministry alarms the governing authorities—Romans, supported by some Jewish leaders—and leads to his arrest, trial, and execution. He is crucified as a criminal and buried. When his followers visit his tomb three days later they find it empty. Mark's gospel ends at this point, but the others tell of miraculous appearances of Jesus which convince his followers that he has been raised from the dead by God. The Book of Acts in the New Testament (written by the author of Luke's gospel) continues the story, recounting how Jesus, having ascended into heaven, pours out his Spirit on his followers on the day of Pentecost, and how the early church comes into being as a result.

Even such a brief summary makes it clear that the shape of the gospels is dictated by their intention: to persuade readers to believe the 'good news' and change their lives accordingly. Though each gospel offers a distinct portrait of Jesus, they agree on key points: that a man who is no mere mortal was born amongst the Jews, that he was uniquely favoured by God, and that those who dedicate their lives to him can experience his supernatural power, and eternal life. In order to persuade readers of the truth of this account, the gospels marshal the most convincing evidence they can: teaching, miracles, resurrection, and the fulfilment of prophecy.

Teaching

The most succinct version of Jesus' teaching is contained in a single gospel verse: 'The time is fulfilled and the reign of God has come near; repent and believe in the good news' (Mark 1:15).

Jesus teaches that far from abandoning his people, God's reign (often translated 'kingdom') is imminent. It is necessary to watch for the signs of the times and be prepared for the new Godly society that is being prepared. Readiness consists in living as if God's will and law are already in force. This should be done by observing the spirit rather than the letter of the Jewish Law—its essence rather than its inessentials. And its essence, Jesus says, is love without limits. God is calling people to love as he loves: with perfect generosity. Those who do the same join the family of God, whose ties and loyalties surpass those of any other form of human association and transcend religious or family ties.

At one level, Jesus is a Jewish teacher with a message for fellow Jews. The followers of an exclusivistic monotheism, their identity was based on the belief that God (Yahweh) had called them out of all the nations, made them His chosen people, granted them the land of Israel for exclusive possession, and given them the Law (Torah) by which to live. In Jesus' day, with Israel under Roman occupation, many were attempting to make sense of this latest episode in the history of God's special people.

At another level, however, Jesus' message can speak to any human being in any time or place. It calls for a personal change of heart. It envisages a universal society bound together by divine love in which the limited human ties of affection based on kinship, cultural identity, and self-interest give way to the unlimited love of God. It calls for an egalitarian kingdom of love without limits. Jesus likens it to a family in which all are brothers and sisters of one another and children of the one Father ('Abba', an informal word for father, is Jesus' preferred name for God). In God's reign, which is already beginning, it will be those who are humble enough to accept their need for God's love and forgiveness who will find that they belong to this new order of things; the proud, self-righteous, and unjust will be revealed for what they are. Thus the first will be last, and the last will be first.

Box 1 Extracts from Jesus' teaching: Matthew 5 and Luke 14

You have heard that it was said, 'You shall love your neighbour and hate your enemy.' But I say to you: Love your enemies and

> pray for those who persecute you, so that you may be sons of
> your Father who is in heaven; for He makes His sun rise on the
> evil and the good, and sends his rain on the just and on the
> unjust.
>
> If anyone comes to me and does not hate his own father and
> mother and wife and children and brothers and sisters, yes, even
> his own life, he cannot be my disciple.

Miracles

Although Jesus' teaching recorded in the gospels is powerful, on
its own it does not establish his unique status because he says
much less about himself than about the loving God he proclaims.
There are relatively few sayings in which he makes explicit
reference to having a unique role and status. Some of these
suggest that he is ordained by God to inaugurate God's rule on
earth. Others have Jesus openly declare that he is the 'Son of God'.
The oldest gospel, the Gospel of John, goes furthest by including
long discourses by Jesus in which he reflects on his divine status.
In addition, there are passages in all gospels in which other people
announce Jesus' unique status—like the centurion who witnesses
his death on a cross and exclaims: 'Truly this man was the Son
of God.'

More important in establishing Jesus' divine status are his
miracles. The gospel narratives are peppered with accounts of
Jesus' miraculous deeds, and linger lovingly over the detail. They
lay great emphasis on the way in which witnesses react with awe
and wonder. Some of the miracles that are recorded involve
human healing, whilst others demonstrate Jesus' control over
natural events—stilling a storm, walking on water, feeding five
thousand. Since God controls the world, the clear implication is
that God was at work in Jesus. Even bystanders who are not
convinced by Jesus' miracles admit that some supernatural power
must be at work—if not God, then Beelzebub, the devil.

Resurrection

However persuasive Jesus' miracles might be, his resurrection is even more impressive, and it is no surprise that three out of four gospels make it their climax (Mark's gospel was amended early on to ensure that it too ended with an account of the risen Christ). Just as the Jewish people believed that only God could work real miracles, so they believed that only God could raise a human being from the dead. There was also widespread belief that God would do this only at the end of time—to inaugurate a more general resurrection which would bring history to an end. Within this worldview, Jesus' resurrection proves that God's power is at work in him in a special way. For those who have ears to hear, it confirms that Jesus has a unique role in God's plan for the world, and that through him the reign of suffering, oppression, and death is about to come to an end.

Fulfilled prophecy

The gospels offer further evidence of Jesus' unique status by showing how much of what they recount happens in fulfilment of prophecies made in the Jewish scriptures. Since God was believed to be in control of history, and the prophets had insight into the direction in which he was leading it, it was important to show that the Hebrew Bible foretells the life, death, and resurrection of Jesus Christ. So intense is the gospels' concern to demonstrate this that scholars now believe that some of their stories about Jesus are actively shaped or even generated by a prophecy.

It was not only Jews who might be convinced by being shown that 'these things took place to fulfil what the prophets foretold.' In the early Christian centuries, the Jewish faith and scriptures were held in high regard by some Romans, who admired their morality and antiquity. By presenting itself as the fulfilment of Jewish hope, Christianity could win a more favourable hearing amongst people who would otherwise dismiss it as a flash-in-the-pan novelty—what we today might refer to as a 'sect' or 'new religious movement'. The logic still holds: if Jesus' life, death, and resurrection are read as a fulfilment of the Jewish scriptures, their authority transfers to him.

Four versions of Jesus

The earliest gospel, Mark, portrays the most human Jesus and the oldest, John, the most thoroughly divine. But all agree that Jesus stood in such a uniquely close relationship to God that he alone crosses the line that separates creatures from the God who made them.

This emphasis on Jesus' divinity is echoed and reinforced in the other documents of the New Testament, including the letters or 'epistles' of Paul. These, written by an early Christian leader to various groups of Christians in the Mediterranean world between about 50 and 70 AD, barely refer to the earthly Jesus. Their focus is the risen Christ, the 'Lord' who dwells in the heavens and is present on earth in His Spirit. Similarly, the later book of Revelation, which ends the New Testament, portrays Jesus as the heavenly lamb who stands by the throne of God and returns to judge the earth at the end of time, precipitating terrible destruction before the heavenly Jerusalem finally descends to earth and God's triumphal reign begins. Once the New Testament is joined to the Old, an entire narrative of history is created. It begins with creation in the first chapters of Genesis, and ends with the restoration of God's purposes—through Christ—in the book of Revelation.

To read the Bible as a whole is thus to be left in no doubt that those who compiled and authorized it in the 4th century were the champions of a version of Christianity that wished to stress the divinity of Christ and the almighty power of the God at whose right hand he now sits. But there were other interpretations open to those who came into contact with Jesus. As they were expressed in the earliest Christian centuries, these interpretations fall into four main groups—and they have set the parameters for interpretation of the figure of Jesus from that day to this.

1. A mere human being

Few of Jesus' Jewish contemporaries considered him anything more than a mortal man. There were lots of itinerant teachers and miracle workers operating in the same area at that time, many of whom proclaimed the coming rule of God. Some were also crucified by the Romans. What made Jesus so special? Gentile (non-Jewish) inhabitants of the Roman Empire were equally sceptical. If even Jesus' own countrymen treated exalted claims about him as far-fetched, who were they to disagree?

Israel in Jesus' time was a small but troublesome region in the Empire, and Jewish radicals were continually inciting their people to rebel against the Romans (such rebellion gave rise to the Jewish wars of 66–70 AD and 132–135 AD). Like Jesus, some of these radicals came from low strata of society and preached a primitive communism. Romans from higher classes were bound to be suspicious. We know from their writings that many found the appeal to miracles and resurrection manipulative, the sighing after another world misguided, and the exclusive worship of a God-man subversive and irrational. There was no doubt Jesus existed, but at best he could be regarded as a charismatic human being.

Modern historical scholarship has also tended to paint a picture of a human Jesus. As information about the Mediterranean world in the 1st century has increased, scholars have been able to make sense of Jesus in his own context. They have found that the oldest layers in the gospels make the least claims about his divinity. The Jesus they portray is a charismatic healer and teacher who initiated an egalitarian social movement. The stories about his supernatural, divine nature come from the era after his death, when followers begin to understand him in terms of fulfilled prophecies and their experience of his continuing presence.

2. A human being exalted by God

Some of those who heard about Jesus were prepared to accept that he was more than human. They thought him special or even unique, but would not go so far as to proclaim him divine.

The idea that God might bless and exalt a man—probably not a woman—was a commonplace in Jewish thought. The scriptures contained many examples: Abraham, Moses, and, above all, the righteous ruler of ancient Israel, King David. Many prophecies focused on a coming messiah who will deliver Israel and restore God's reign. Though there are different visions, the messiah is generally viewed as a mighty man anointed by God.

Given the heightened climate of messianic expectation in Jesus' day, it was relatively easy for some of his earliest Jewish followers to view him as the long-awaited messiah. The Greek word 'Christ' which translates the Hebrew word 'Messiah' is one of the first titles associated with Jesus, possibly during his own lifetime. We know that there were many early Christian groups who remained faithful to the Jewish law and its ritual observances, and who continued to consider themselves Jews. What set these 'Jewish Christians' apart from their fellows was their belief that the messiah had appeared in Jesus of Nazareth and would shortly return to inaugurate God's kingdom. The New Testament tells us that Paul came into conflict with such Christians when he took the gospel to gentiles and relaxed the demands of the Jewish Law, including circumcision. Though Paul's strategy eventually won the day, there is evidence that groups of Jewish Christians continued to exist for many centuries. Their interpretation of Jesus as a man exalted by God also found expression in the early Christian doctrine of 'adoptionism'—the belief that Jesus Christ was a righteous human being who had been adopted and anointed by God.

Even today there are many who are prepared to grant that Jesus was special in God's eyes, but who draw the line at considering him divine. This is the official view of Islam, for example. Jesus is mentioned many times in the Qur'an, and depicted as a miracle-working prophet chosen by God to spread his message. Though human, God exalted Jesus into heaven (he was not crucified and resurrected as Christians claim), and he will return on the day of judgement.

3. A divine being who inspires others to become divine

The reason many Jews and, later, Muslims could accept that Jesus was special but not divine is that their faiths are strictly monotheistic. It is possible that a human being can be called by God, exalted by God, adopted by God—even taken up to heaven— but there can only be one God. In Hellenistic culture, however, the boundaries between divine and human were more blurry. The Roman Empire in Jesus' day—including much Jewish culture— still drew inspiration from the cultural legacy of the ancient Greeks ('Hellenes'). It knew many deities, not just one. Gods and goddesses were depicted as larger-than-life human beings in whom human virtues and vices were magnified. Since the deities often took human form and mingled with mortals, it was easy enough to fit a divine Jesus into such a scheme.

Many different groups in the early centuries of the Christian era saw Jesus in this way. Recently discovered non-canonical scriptures, most notably from Nag Hammadi in Upper Egypt, have enlarged our understanding. Though later classified as 'gnostic' and heretical by followers of 'orthodox' Christianity, they were more diverse in belief and organization than these blanket terms suggest. Nevertheless, many shared the view that Jesus imparted a special wisdom or 'gnosis' which enabled others to find and free their own divine nature. Rather than viewing him as a god to be worshipped, they viewed him as a being who had attained divinity and could help others do the same. Some gnostic groups were ascetic. They viewed the body as lower than the spirit, and taught that Jesus did not really take human flesh but only appeared to do so—a view called 'docetism' from the Greek meaning 'to seem'. A variation was offered by the 4th century Christian teacher Arius, who argued that Jesus had a quasi-divine status somewhere between a man and God (see Chapter 4). Both docetism and Arianism would be condemned by later Christianity as heretical.

> ### Box 2 Extract from the Gospel of Thomas (Saying 3)
>
> Jesus says, 'If your leaders say to you, "Look, the Father's rule is in the sky," then the birds of the sky will precede you. If they say to you, "It is in the sea," then the fish will precede you. Rather the Father's rule is inside you and outside you. When you know yourselves, then you will be known, and you will understand that you are children of the living Father. But if you do not know yourselves, you live in poverty, and you are the poverty.'

4. The unique God-man

The views of Jesus outlined so far fall along a spectrum with those which interpret him as merely human, or more-man-than-God, at one end, and those which interpret him as more-God-than-man at the other. The view which gradually became established as the orthodox Christian interpretation holds together the beliefs that Jesus is truly God *and* truly human.

It is possible to glimpse this view coming into being in the earliest documents of the New Testament, the letters of Paul. Paul was Jewish and monotheistic. He believes that there is only one creator God and that all creatures are subordinate to him. This rules out the gnostic route for Paul, for it is impossible to affirm that humans can be reunited with their divine source. But neither can Paul accept an adoptionist view, for he believes that Jesus is unique.

Paul did not know the human Jesus, but he had an overwhelmingly powerful experience of the risen Christ which changed the course of his life, and to which he refers in his letters. This convinced him that Jesus is connected to God in a way that no other human being ever has been, can be, or will be. Paul speaks of Jesus as 'Christ' and as 'Lord'—a term he also uses for God. He thinks of Christ as the timeless wisdom of God, by and through whom all things were made. He was with God from the beginning of time, and is the image of the perfect divine humanity which gives the whole creation its meaning, purpose, and destiny.

Unlike gnosticism, the Pauline view presents human beings not with the challenge of realizing their own divinity in imitation of Jesus, but with the duty of grateful submission to the Lord. Although they have no natural ability to become Christlike, by supernatural grace they may become what Paul calls 'sons by adoption'. For Paul, the ritual of water baptism symbolizes the death of the old self and the birth of a new person. After baptism, Paul says, 'it is no longer I who live, but Christ who lives in me.' The baptized do not become gods in their own right, but members of 'the body of Christ' under the headship of the Lord. Their transformation begins on earth but will culminate in their resurrection from the dead. Christ is divine, and human beings are saved by being incorporated into him in the power of the Spirit and by the grace of God.

In this view, which would be refined and systematized by later Christian thinkers, Jesus is the unique God-man. Though truly human, he is divine in a way no other human being ever can be—other than by the gift of incorporation into his risen life. In much actual Christian practice his humanity, though affirmed, tends to be subsumed and subordinated to his divinity, just as it is in the equally exalted view of Christ as the 'Word of God' which is developed in John's gospel. The distinction between God and humanity is preserved, as is the necessity of human subordination. Humans are saved not by their own powers, but by the power of God.

These are not easy ideas. Christians throughout the centuries have struggled to hold together the orthodox view that Jesus, the God-man, is fully human and fully divine. In practice, his divinity has often overwhelmed his humanity. Jesus is depicted as so all-knowing and perfect that he seems nothing like a real human being. This is a kind of docetism, in which Jesus only *appears* to be human—as in the line in the popular carol 'Hark the Herald Angels' which says 'veiled in flesh the Godhead see.' Some non-Christians see the sheer difficulty of the orthodox view of Jesus as the 'God-man' as a fundamental weakness of the religion, but orthodox Christians see it as a witness to the mystery of God's close relation with humanity.

The maleness of Christ

One issue not discussed in early Christian reflections on Jesus is his being male. After the advent of feminism, however, it became hard to ignore. Is it significant that the God-man is male? Could Jesus have been female, and are images of 'him' as female heretical or acceptable?

For some, Christ's maleness is a serious stumbling block. It reinforces the idea that God is male, an idea which Christianity reinforces by referring to God with the male pronoun, and depicting him as a Father, King, and so on. Then it makes this even worse by implying that if a human can be divine, only a male can be. As Mary Daly, a feminist theologian who later rejected Christianity, famously said: 'if God is male, then male is God.'

Christians may respond by saying that both God and Christ transcend gender, and that it makes no sense to think of either one as male or female—these are just images to help us, and all images fall short. If that is the case, then Jesus' maleness may be purely contingent—in theory he could just as well have been a woman, though in practice a woman could not have been a public figure in his day and age. What matters is Christ's humanity, not his being male.

Another way of responding is to point out that women have been crucial to the spread and success of Christianity. Jesus appears to have treated women as equals, and his message had an egalitarian emphasis. Early Christian communities not only attracted women, but in some cases had women leaders, patrons, prophets, healers, and teachers. Different early Christian groups probably appealed for various reasons—some because they were very positive about women's domestic roles, others because their asceticism allowed women to avoid marriage and family altogether. But insofar as data is available it seems that women have been more active within Christianity than men in most historical eras, even though they have not held equal power.

It is even possible that Jesus' maleness is more attractive to women than to men. Is it not more natural for heterosexual women to love and adore a male divinity than for heterosexual men to do the same? A good deal of Christian piety has a strongly erotic tinge, with Christ being envisaged as a heavenly bridegroom, for example. In contemporary evangelical piety many women still engage in romance with Jesus—as one said, 'Jesus alone understands me, loves me, and forgives me.'

Obviously, Christians cannot use both the arguments rehearsed here—that Jesus' maleness is important and has consequences for Christian devotion, and that it is irrelevant because the God-man transcends gender. Given the importance of images and symbols in Christianity, the first argument seems more plausible. Christians have generally viewed both God and Jesus as male, and this has no doubt had consequences which include reinforcement of an enduring inequality between men and women. This also means that although Christianity may have had advantages in attracting women in pre-feminist societies, it may lose those advantages when a feminist perspective is widely accepted.

Conclusion

A religion which has a God-man at its centre is bound to be a religion full of tension, complication and creativity. Jesus Christ unifies, but he also divides. At some point in history each and every one of the interpretations of Jesus discussed in this chapter—and more besides—would find its champions and win its supporters. Some Christians have been attracted by the 'Jesus' in Jesus Christ—the human figure who teaches, inspires, and dies for the cause in which he believes. Others are drawn to the 'Christ' in Christ Jesus—the divine figure who performs miracles, fulfils prophecies, rises from the dead, and is God. The orthodox position is to keep both in tension, framing Jesus as the ultimate boundary-crosser who abolishes division between humans and God; but the human is always in danger of being overshadowed by the divine. The battles between these different understandings of Jesus, and the communities and institutions established around them, have shaped the course of Christianity, and sometimes of whole societies, for over two millennia.

Chapter 2
Beliefs, rituals, and narratives

Having considered how the figure of Jesus was interpreted, we can take the story further by looking at how depictions of him developed, and how they fit into the broader scheme of Christian rituals and symbols. Later chapters explain how the elements of Christianity discussed here were developed in different branches of Christianity. In Eastern Christianity, for example, less emphasis is placed on sin than in Western churches, and in some forms of Christianity the Holy Spirit has a much more central place than others. In this chapter, however, we can turn down the volume on such differences in order to introduce common themes in the Christian repertoire.

God and history

As Christianity developed, its leaders tried to maintain unity not only by creating a canon of scripture, the Bible, but by formulating creeds (authoritative statements of belief), theologies (attempts to articulate the Christian faith using words and concepts), and liturgies (the formulations which guide communal worship of God). At first these things were not neatly separated. One of the earliest Western creeds, the Apostles' Creed, dating from the late 5th century, illustrates this. In its structure, it begins with God the Father, then tells the story of Jesus Christ, and ends with the Holy Spirit, the Church, and the hope of resurrection. As such, it offers both a coherent 'salvation history' and an embryonic version of the Christian doctrine of the Trinity according to which God is both one (monotheism) and three (Trinitarianism). It also became an element of the liturgy used in many Western Churches.

Box 3 The Apostles' Creed

I believe in God, the Father almighty,
creator of heaven and earth.
I believe in Jesus Christ, God's only Son, our Lord,
who was conceived by the Holy Spirit,
born of the Virgin Mary,
suffered under Pontius Pilate,
was crucified, died, and was buried;
he descended into hell.
On the third day he rose again;
he ascended into heaven,
he is seated at the right hand of the Father,
and he will come to judge the living and the dead.
I believe in the Holy Spirit,
the holy Catholic Church,
The communion of saints,
the forgiveness of sins,
the resurrection of the body,
and the life everlasting. Amen.

One of the main ways in which the Christian account of salvation history was made coherent was by connecting what happened at the beginning of creation with what Christ had done towards its end. Within this scheme, Jesus was viewed as the 'second Adam'. Whereas the first Adam—the first man, according to Genesis— had closed the doors of paradise to those who followed after him by eating the forbidden fruit offered to him by Eve, the second Adam—Christ—has thrown the doors open. He has defeated both sin and death, and those who follow him can share in his triumph. Mary, the mother of Jesus, was also interpreted by many Christians within this scheme—as a second Eve who rights the wrongs of the first.

Over time, Christians developed many ways of explaining how Christ saves. These were expressed in theories of 'atonement'. Some theories said that Christ had defeated the devil and his angels, others that he was a sacrifice or sin-offering to God (the 'lamb of God'), still others that humans are saved by entering into mystical unity with the heavenly Christ through the action of the Holy Spirit. What most theories had in common was the idea that Christ can save because he both shares our humanity and transcends it. Since human beings are too corrupted to save themselves, God intervenes through him on our behalf.

Different accounts of salvation implied different things about the nature of the relationships between Father, Son, and Holy Spirit—the three persons of the Trinity. Did the Father send the Son, who in turn sent the Holy Spirit? That made the Trinity sound like a hierarchy in which the three members are not truly equal. To avoid this, some said that the Holy Spirit is the Spirit of both Father and Son and proceeds from both, that each indwells the other, and that all three are co-eternal. The heated debates about these issues are discussed in more detail in later chapters. However they are resolved, the doctrine of the Trinity gives Christianity great flexibility in its understanding of God. As we will see, different varieties of the religion emphasize one aspect of God more than others. Sometimes God the Father has primacy—perhaps as a stern judge or as a more loving figure. Sometimes Jesus is more important—perhaps by way of a living relationship with him experienced as the heart of a Christian life. And sometimes it is the Holy Spirit who comes to the fore—with the indwelling Spirit, or gifts of the Spirit (*charismata*), being regarded as the true marks of a Christian.

Images of Christ

Like all religions, Christianity revolves around symbols and images as well as narratives and beliefs. Although it has produced some depictions of God the Father—usually as an elderly, bearded man—there is a reticence about creating such images, perhaps inherited from Judaism, and shared with Islam. The Holy Spirit is also a difficult subject for visual representation, not least because it is said to be invisible. Images of the Spirit as a dove or rays of light are the most conventional. But Christianity compensates for these difficulties by offering artists the male and female, human and divine, angelic and diabolical characters which people the vivid stories of the Old and New Testaments and apocryphal books.

Just as Christian thinking about Jesus developed gradually, so images of him took time to emerge. By the 4th century the figure of a slim, pale, bearded, robed, long-haired, ethereal figure emerged, and it has dominated the Christian imagination ever since. This Jesus has a human face, but it is no ordinary face. His expression is impassive, his gaze direct, his divinity signalled by an aura or halo. His power is manifest in his bearing—often seated on a throne, with a hand raised in blessing, sometimes with a book of law. At first he is located beyond the mundane world in an empty, dimensionless golden space. Similarly, Mary is depicted in early Christian iconography as serene, powerful, and loving, either on her own or holding the infant Christ. What we have are icons rather than pictures, magical images that offer direct access to the mysterious divine power they represent.

The icon of 'Christ Pantocrator', Christ the ruler of all things, depicted in Figure 2, is found above the altar in some Eastern churches. To see it you look upwards, far above the earth and the human condition. There the all-powerful saviour looks down from the heavens. The effect is not only to induce awe, humility, and reverence but to inspire joy, hope, and gratitude. In entering such

2. Christ Pantocrator

a church one steps out of the mundane world and is given a
foretaste of the higher spiritual reality that surrounds it—the
world of Jesus, Mary, and the saints. More real than this world, it
can be accessed by the faithful not only after death but here and
now—by receiving the church's sacraments, participating in its
rituals, hearing its music, viewing its dazzling images, and obeying
its authority.

3. *Crucifixion*, by Matthias Grünewald (1500–8)

The first images of a more human Jesus emerge in the West in the early middle ages. They show him suffering and dying upon a cross. No longer is his body upright and victorious as in earlier depictions, but twisted, bleeding, and broken—as in Figure 3. Such images encouraged believers to meditate on the suffering of the Christ, the human sinfulness that caused such suffering, and the amazing love of a God-man prepared to die for those who killed him. Paradoxically, the more the suffering of Christ was emphasized, the more it could become a mark of his unique divine status rather than his common humanity. The middle ages also saw the growth of intense devotion to Mary, who is depicted in some medieval images as a towering goddess-like figure, protecting and sheltering her devotees.

The Renaissance of the 13th to 15th centuries often depicted Christ and Mary in more human ways. So-called because it involved a re-naissance ('re-birth') of classical culture, this European cultural movement revived the ancient Graeco-Roman theme of the dignity of the human mind and body. Since it was a Christian as much as a classical movement, this dignity was often expressed through images of Jesus. In the work of Giotto, for example, Jesus, Mary, and other characters from the Christian story appear as human not merely by virtue of their suffering, but in their ability to express the full range of emotions in three-dimensional bodies of flesh and blood. In Giotto's frescoes even angels have feelings; like Jesus' devoted human followers, they weep and beat their breasts as they behold the death of Christ. Later Renaissance art would go even further towards the humanization of Jesus, sometimes depicting him naked and with male genitalia—here sexuality is seen as a part of human perfection rather than a mark of its fall.

The modern period introduced new tendencies. One was to moralize biblical stories, and to depict the 'holy family' as a model human family, as in Figure 4. With the invention of cheap colour printing, devotional images produced for popular consumption assumed new importance. In Roman Catholic depictions of *The Sacred Heart*, Jesus literally lays bare his heart to those who would love or scorn him (Figure 5); in Holman Hunt's famous allegory *The Light of the World* he knocks on the door that symbolizes the human soul and that can only be opened from within (Figure 6); in Warner Sallman's *Head of Christ* he is brooding and intense

4. *The Holy Family with a Little Bird,* by Murillo (*c.*1650)

(Figure 7). Women were often the most important consumers of such images.

Sin

The more emphasis Christianity placed on the importance of Christ and the Church, the more it had to explain what problem they existed to solve. The answer was sin. The bigger the sin, the greater the need of salvation. 'O felix culpa...' exclaims the Latin mass of the Roman Catholic Church: 'Oh happy sin which has received as its reward so great and so good a redeemer.'

The Bible talks about sin, but it was the early Christian bishop and theologian Augustine (354–430) who gave it new force by placing it in the context of a powerful narrative: the story of the Fall. Augustine based his account on Genesis 3 which recounts how the first human beings, Adam and Eve, disobey God and are cast out of paradise—east of Eden. The story can be interpreted

5. *The Sacred Heart of Jesus.* Image on a popular card (*c.*1900)

6. *The Light of the World*, by Holman Hunt (1900–4)

7. *Head of Christ,* by Warner Sallman (1941)

in a number of ways. For Jewish interpreters and Christian theologians in the East, the story can be read in a positive as well as a negative light—as a coming of age. Augustine disagrees. For him it is utterly negative. Adam and Eve are disobedient, immodest, proud, and greedy. They have lost the human race its place in paradise, corrupted their God-given nature, and passed on the corruption to all their descendants. Augustine believed that

Adam and Eve were the real, biological parents of the human race, and that their sin was transmitted to all their descendants—the whole human race—through sexual reproduction.

Augustine's account profoundly affected the way in which Christians in the West thought about themselves. It gave a negative cast to self-understanding. Since humans are held responsible for all the bad things in life, their suffering is compounded by guilt. And there is nothing they can do without God's intervention. Born with a fatal flaw, they have inherited an inbuilt pride, disobedience, and concupiscence (the overwhelming of reason and self-control by the appetites and passions). Human beings are out of control, unable to obey either the dictates of their own reason and conscience or those of God himself. Nowhere is this more obvious than in the way in which the human body controls the mind and leads us astray; for Augustine and those he influenced, sexual desire is the most powerful symptom of the Fall.

Not every Western theologian was prepared to go all the way with Augustine. Some, like Aquinas (see Chapter 3), did not believe that human reason had been so utterly corrupted that it was unable to discern the existence of God or distinguish basic right from wrong. But they accepted the main thrust of Augustine's interpretation, and endorsed the view that humans are powerless to save themselves. The practical implications were clear. Human beings are damaged goods. They cannot save themselves. If men and women are not to live wretched lives on earth and still more wretched lives in the hell that awaits them after death, they require the assistance of the heavenly saviour Jesus Christ, and of his church on earth.

Salvation

As it became an increasingly powerful institution, the church insisted that it was the only route to salvation, and it offered very practical ways in which salvation could be secured. It taught that

God's grace is mediated to humanity by two channels, Word and sacrament. Both are to be received in the communal setting of Christian worship, presided over by clergy.

Although different forms of Christianity lay more stress on one or the other, all Christian worship offers either Word or sacrament or some combination of both. The Word is, primarily, the Bible, but also exposition and teaching. A sacrament is a material object which symbolizes and transmits divine power. Although the Catholic Church would eventually recognize seven sacraments (baptism, eucharist, penance, confirmation, ordination, marriage, extreme unction), there are two which are recognized by nearly all Christian churches: baptism and eucharist (the latter also called 'mass', 'holy communion', and 'the Lord's supper'). Both baptism and eucharist are believed to have been instituted by Jesus. Although they were formalized into solemn rituals by the churches, in their basic elements they could not be simpler: a washing in water, and a sharing of bread and wine.

Christians believe that in baptism an individual is 'born again', not into the world but into the church, not by natural birth but by supernatural re-birth. The transition is marked by an immersion in water symbolizing entry into the womb or the grave, as well as a washing and cleansing. The Christian significance of this ritual is expressed by the language of 'washing in the blood of the lamb' (Christ being likened to a sacrificial lamb), and in the metaphor of dying to sin in order to live in Christ. The ritual brings Christians new life in several senses. First, they are no longer under the power of the devil and evil spirits but under the Lordship of Christ—a transition that is also marked by anointing with oil. Second, they live according to a new set of standards—not of the world but of Christ and his church. Third, they let go of their old mortal life and begin to live a new risen life in Christ—they are born again, into eternal life.

The eucharist repeats, reiterates, and reinforces baptism. The simple act of sharing a meal has an obvious significance in binding together those who participate. For Christians this significance is extended by virtue of the fact that Christ, at the last supper he ate with his disciples, is said to have commanded them to 'do this in remembrance of me.' What is more, the bread and wine are understood as symbols of the sacrifice he made after eating the meal: giving his flesh and blood for the salvation of the human race. The symbolism is powerful: those who participate are being nourished by Christ's own body. It becomes part of them and they become part of Him, as well as being drawn into closer relationship with one another. Since Christ's death on the cross is often interpreted as a sacrificial offering to God, so the eucharist is understood as a symbol or even a repetition of this unique sacrifice of the beloved Son.

What Christianity does, in other words, is to take 'nature' and make it sacred by bringing it into relation with the grace of God in Christ. Thus the 'natural' stages of life—from cradle to grave— are 'Christianized', starting with baptism at birth and ending with a Christian funeral at death—a prelude to what awaits the individual beyond the grave. Christianity does the same with time, taking some of the stages of nature's seasons and rhythms, and bringing them into relation with the life and death of Christ. As Figure 8 shows, the Christian year is organized around Christ's birth (Christmas), his death and resurrection (Good Friday and Easter), and other lesser feasts and fasts. The Christian week pivots around the day on which Christ was raised from the dead (Sunday). And the whole of historical time is dated around the birth of Christ (BC and AD). Thus both personal life and social life, and indeed the whole of creation, is conformed ever more closely to the life, death, and resurrection of the God-man.

Holy Spirit

The Holy Spirit is the active presence of God in the world, a free-floating power which 'blows where it wills', and can overwhelm and possess human beings (as can evil spirits). This

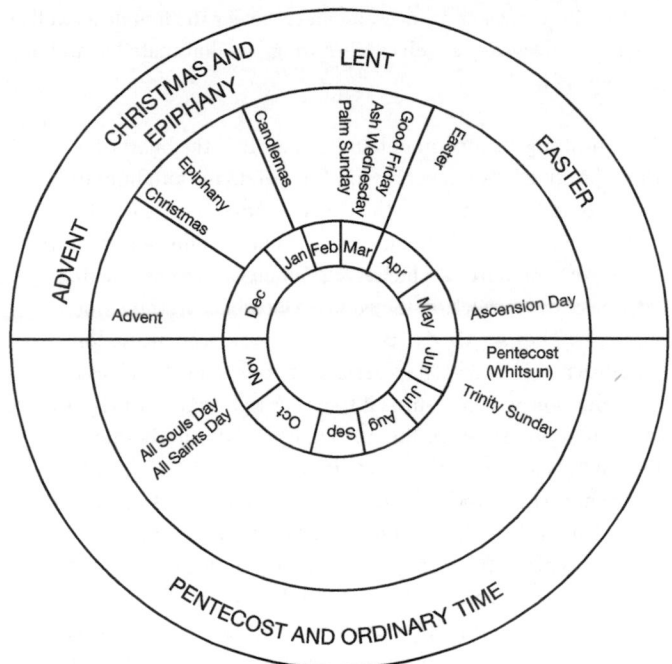

8. The Christian year

makes the Spirit a potentially dangerous and uncontrollable
element, especially for church authorities. Because anyone
can claim to be inspired by the Spirit, it became necessary for
churches to establish ways of testing and limiting its operation.
One way to keep the Spirit within authorized channels is to claim
that it is uniquely present in the Word and the sacraments, which
can only be consecrated (made sacred) by a priest. Another way is
to insist that, since it is the Spirit of Christ, it can only inspire
people to act in Christ-like ways. But to some extent the Holy
Spirit remains the rogue element in Christianity, the sacred in
a form which is hard to pin down. It is always open to ordinary
women and men to claim its inspiration, and thus to lay hold of
God's power. And because the Spirit is invisible and eludes

35

capture in words and images, it can empower the female as well as the male, the weak as well as the strong, the dominated as well as the powerful.

The Spirit injects movement and change into the heart of Christianity. Christian representations of divine and human reality tend to be rather static. God is changeless. He creates a world which is fully formed, and which needs only to be restored to the perfection from which it fell. When Christians imagine goodness and perfection they tend to look back in time, not forwards. They see Christ as the second Adam, the Kingdom as Paradise regained or a 'new Jerusalem', the ideal church as a 're-formation' which returns it to its earliest origins. Christians have often preferred tradition to change, and churches have tended to be conservative. The Spirit introduces a different, more suppressed, theme in Christianity: that God is present in and through change, working to 'make all things new'. Where Christians have embraced the Spirit most enthusiastically, the consequences have often been disruptive. As we will see in Chapter 4, for example, the Quakers, who have a very strong emphasis on the Spirit as an 'inner light' within every person, dispense with priests, sacraments, and scriptures, and have a history of radical social and political action.

This is not to imply that Christianity is always content with the world as it is. Far from it. In looking above to the heavenly Father, Christianity also looks beyond. It cherishes a vision of perfection—not the way things are, but the way God wills them to be. This vision is summed up in Christ, and enacted in the rituals Christians perform when they come together. In the church there is a foretaste of heaven, and in the indwelling Spirit there is eternal life here and now. Christian ritual anticipates what lies beyond. Such 'beyondness' may be thought of in spatial terms (heaven, a higher realm) or temporal ones (the coming Kingdom of God, the end of the world). Consequently, Christians say both that the saved go to heaven when they die and that they will be resurrected at the end of time. Christians often say that they are 'in the world, but not of it'. Whilst they may embrace political hopes and plans, they tend to be sceptical about attempts to construct heavens on earth.

Conclusion

What sets Christianity apart from other monotheisms is its emphasis on the unique God-man in which the might, majesty, and mercy of God are made visible and accessible to mortals. This saviour becomes the focus of a new community—the church—with distinctive rituals, beliefs, and scriptures. The promise is that all who join and receive God's Spirit through Word and sacraments can be saved. This is made vivid by being wrapped into a story about how the human race was created, fell, and is redeemed by Christ. Until the modern period, many Christians understood this as a literal account of history. Today it is more common to understand it as the framework within which their lives are lived. Whichever way, Christians' task and privilege is to play their part in a wider drama of creation and redemption.

Chapter 3
The spread of Christianity

From its fragile origins within a small country under imperial occupation, Christianity had, by the 19th century, grown to become the world's largest religion. Although Christians have explained this success in terms of God's action, few would deny that alliances with worldly power were also involved. This chapter charts Christianity's growth and spread, and explains how a fringe movement turned into a 'world religion'.

Early growth

There is no way of knowing how many followers Jesus attracted in his own lifetime, but we are probably talking about a tiny number, including some of his own family. Jesus started a reform movement within the Jewish religion, he did not establish a new religion or any of the institutional elements it requires—formal rituals and organizational structures, for example. After his death what was left were memories of him, experience of his living presence, and small groups of people mobilized around these. Many early followers were Jewish, but some began to drift from Jewish practices, particularly in communities which started to attract non-Jews.

We can glimpse a stage in the transitional process from movement to organization in Paul's letters. Paul was a Jew who had become an 'apostle', a full-time witness to Christ who ministered to several Christian communities around the Mediterranean. Their variety is clear from the advice he gives them. Some still practise in a very egalitarian way, but in others it is clear that a few individuals, including Paul himself, are starting to claim special authority as leaders. Some groups remain strictly observant of Jewish Law, whilst others are much more Hellenistic, with tendencies towards what would later be labelled gnosticism (introduced in the last chapter). Paul tries to steer a middle course between the 'Judaizers' and the 'gnostics'. He tells the former that Christ has come to fulfil the Law and that the Spirit sets them free from strict observance, and the latter that the gift of the Spirit does not allow complete licence, for not everyone has the same authority, and it is necessary to build up the body of Christ in an orderly way.

As time went on and Jesus' contemporaries began to die, teachings by and about him began to be written down. Leadership, which at first had been loosely based on a community's willingness to accept an individual's gifts and abilities, gradually came to be more formally organized. Some communities accepted the principle of 'apostolic succession' according to which authority was passed down a chain of men who claimed a direct connection back to Jesus and his disciples. In order to make sure that the purity of this line was safeguarded, those who belonged to it chose their successors carefully and authorized them through a laying on of hands—which gradually developed into a formal rite of priestly 'ordination'. As well as concentrating power amongst a few, apostolic succession helped establish greater uniformity of teaching and belief.

Although both women and men exercised leadership roles in early Christian communities, apostolic succession and the priestly office were reserved for men alone. A few of the epistles (letters) in the New Testament comment that women should not teach— suggesting that some did so. The arguments against women's equal participation could be biblical—for example, that Eve had led Adam astray—or could appeal to domestic order and the view that wives should be subordinate to husbands. Also influential was the Hellenistic view of gender supported by the philosopher Aristotle, which held that men developed in the womb for longer than women, and were stronger and closer to the perfection of human nature (and so to God) as a result. There was clearly a struggle over the issue, for later 'orthodox' condemnations of gnostic groups often single out the fact that they allow women to behave inappropriately, and some apocryphal scriptures give women a more prominent role than the books which were collected into the New Testament.

It is clear nonetheless that both Jewish and Roman women were attracted to the growing Christian movement in large numbers, and that their energies and enthusiasm were a major factor in its success. Class also seems to have played a part. Rather than attracting the poorest of the poor, early Christianity probably appealed to a growing middle class which included fairly prosperous traders, merchants, and craftsmen, who moved freely within the Roman Empire. Paul, for example, was a Jewish tent-maker who had Roman citizenship. For both groups—women and the mobile middle-class citizens—Christianity offered advantages. It was much easier to join than the Jewish religion, and it gave greater opportunities for leadership, community, and welfare support than did much Graeco-Roman religion. Some forms, like the emerging monastic tradition discussed in Chapter 5, allowed women and men to escape from family responsibilities altogether, whilst others affirmed family bonds and dignified domestic roles. Christians looked after one another's needs and provided a life-line for groups like widows and orphans. Moreover, the religion offered the dazzling promise of eternal life—here and now in the Spirit, and thereafter in everlasting life.

By the 2nd century some of these lines of development were coming together to form the basis of 'Church Christianity', the most successful form of early Christianity, whose development is described in the next chapter. Its advocates called it 'catholic' (which means 'universal') and 'orthodox' (which means 'right belief'). By presenting itself as the one true, universal form of Christianity, this type of Christianity positioned alternative versions of the faith as deviations, and their followers as gnostics, schismatics, and heretics. Its claim to catholicity was given strong institutional underpinning by its line of male apostolic succession, its increasingly unified set of ritual practices, and its emerging canon of scripture and creeds. A hierarchy of leadership developed in which 'bishops' had oversight over 'priests', who in turn had authority over 'deacons' who were responsible for pastoral care and other services. Those who belonged to this 'three-fold order' were classified as 'clergy' in distinction from 'laity'. All these developments helped enforce discipline within Church Christianity and bind its many communities together under a single head—God the Father, represented on earth by the bishop and other clergy.

> ### Box 4 Extract from Ignatius (c.35–107 AD), 'To the Smyrneans'
>
> Avoid divisions, as the beginning of evil. Follow, all of you, the bishop, as Jesus Christ followed the Father...Let that eucharist be considered valid which is under the bishop or him to whom he commits it...Whatsover [the bishop] approves, that is well pleasing to God.

The growing dominance of the Catholic kind of Church Christianity was undergirded by the support of the Roman Emperor Constantine. Prior to the year 313 in which he promulgated the 'Edict of Milan' granting toleration to all religions in the empire, Christians had faced sporadic persecution by Roman rulers, mainly because some refused to sacrifice and show loyalty to the Empire, its gods, and its rulers. In a world of tolerant pantheism, some viewed this kind of exclusive monotheism as dangerous and fanatical. Yet there is more to the story of the Empire's relation to Christianity than persecution, for there were many Romans who were sympathetic to this new religion, and a good number who joined it. What is more, Christianity appears to have been particularly successful within the capital of the western empire, Rome, and to have attracted some noble and high-born Romans to its ranks. Since it did not disrupt Roman life and institutions too greatly, other than by calling for a more rigorous personal morality and an abandonment of all other forms of worship, this is not as surprising as it might seem. When it came to radical issues like questioning the patriarchal nature of the family or the slave-based economy of the Roman Empire, Catholic Christianity was silent. Its advocates were concerned to convince the Romans that Christians were trustworthy, moral, and loyal citizens whose presence in the empire could only strengthen it.

There were many advantages for an ambitious Roman Emperor like Constantine in improving relations with this kind of hierarchical, male-led, unified Christianity. This, after all, was a religion which understood power as the possession of an Almighty God on high, and it was far better that the Emperor be understood as God's deputy on earth, upholding divine justice, than as a tyrant whose position was based on force. What is more, Christianity could help the Emperor achieve a dream of unifying and extending the Empire. When Constantine turned to Christianity he was in the process of disposing of co-emperors with whom he had to share power, and his next plan was to move eastwards to conquer the mighty Persian Empire. Church Christianity could further his ambitions because it also harboured hopes of conquering the world by bringing together all nations under the rule of God. By establishing communities across the empire and beyond, and by bringing them together under centralized leadership, it had already taken important steps in this direction. It had already established communities in the lands that Constantine longed to conquer, including Persia.

The emerging orthodox, Catholic Church therefore accepted imperial patronage willingly. In the ancient world, religions without political backing were always vulnerable and exposed, and once Constantine and his successors threw their weight behind this form of Christianity, its success was virtually assured. Not only did patronage bring enormous financial and legal advantages, but bishops could now call upon the might of the state to oppose their rivals. These included not only competing forms of Christianity ('heresy'), but Hellenistic religion and culture as well ('paganism'). With the aura of official approval, bishops became figures of considerable worldly as well as spiritual power within their dioceses (an area of jurisdiction modelled on a unit of imperial administration). Christian writers like Eusebius of Caesarea (*c*.260–*c*.340) were quick to characterize Constantine as 'the deputy of Christ', and eager to insist that the alliance of church and empire was part of God's providential plan for the world—part of the unfolding narrative of salvation history.

> **Box 5 Extract from Eusebius, 'Oration', 3.5–6**
>
> Invested as he is with a semblance of heavenly sovereignty, [the Emperor] directs his gaze above, and frames his earthly rule according to the pattern of the divine original, feeling strength in its conformity to the monarchy of God . . . And surely monarchy far transcends every other constitution and form of government: for that democratic equality of power, which is its opposite, may rather be described as anarchy and disorder.

Eastern Christianity

Despite Christianity's growth in Rome, it was in the eastern rather than the western part of the Roman Empire that its success would be greatest in the period of late antiquity. To view Christianity as a Western religion is to read later history back into early Christianity. In fact its greatest expansion and most important centres were first established in the Greek-speaking East, not the Latin-speaking West. This was reinforced by Constantine's transfer of the imperial capital from Rome to Constantinople (previously called Byzantium, today called Istanbul) between 324 and 330 AD, and by the gradual transformation of the classical Roman empire into the Christian Byzantine empire, which survived until 1453.

If Catholic Christianity was to help Constantine realize his ambitions, however, he first had to deal with growing tensions between different factions within it, tensions which were mobilizing around theological disputes about the nature of the God-man. Matters came to a head over the views of Arius (d. 366) from Alexandria in Egypt, who proposed that Jesus should be understood neither as God nor man, but as a quasi-divine being whose status hovered somewhere between the two. He maintained that since Jesus was created by the Father there was a time 'when he was not', and that the Son must therefore be of lesser status than the Father.

Though the Arian position was widely accepted, opponents like Athanasius of Alexandria (c.296–373) believed that it struck at the very roots of a powerful Catholic Church. If Jesus was not truly God *and* truly human, he would not be able to assume human nature and save humanity by bringing it within the scope of divinity. Christianity would become a second-rate religion that put human beings in touch not with the exclusive mediator between God and man, but with a middle-ranking deity. Athanasius and other church leaders realized that the unique status of sacraments, priesthood, and Church depended on the unique status of the God-man.

So serious was the dispute that in 325 Constantine called a council at Nicaea in present-day Turkey to settle it. Bishops assembled and scholars gave their views. In the end the opinion of Athanasius and his supporters was affirmed as orthodox, and Arius was anathematized. The Council drew up one of the most influential and widely accepted of Christian creeds, the Creed of Nicaea. Its key clause stated that Jesus was 'homoousios': of one (homo) substance (ousios) with the Father. In other words: he shared the very essence of divinity. He was the God-man.

> **Box 6 Extract from the Nicaean creed**
>
> We believe in One God, the Father, Almighty...
>
> And in One Lord Jesus Christ, the Son of God, begotten of the Father, Only-begotten, that is, from the substance of the Father;
>
> God from God, Light from Light, Very God from Very God...
>
> And those who say 'There was when he was not'...The Catholic and Apostolic church anathematizes.

Arianism did not die out overnight, not least because it was adopted by some of the so-called barbarian tribes on the fringes of the Empire. But the Council of Nicaea was nevertheless the most successful of the several councils that would later be called to settle other contentious points of doctrine and church order. Later councils found it increasingly difficult to establish unity. The influential Council of Chalcedon of 451 clarified what had been implied at Nicaea by saying that Jesus was 'very God and very man', but failed to win as much widespread assent. Two large portions of the Church split from the imperial Catholic Church at this point. These are the so-called 'non-Chalcedonian churches': the Nestorian churches of Antioch, Persia, and further east, and the Monophysite churches of North Africa and Syria. Remnants of both survive. By insisting on creedal conformity on the part of all its members, the imperially-supported Church had managed to maintain unity, but at the price of alienating large parts of its constituency.

In the end, political and religious setbacks foiled Constantine's plans to conquer Persia, and non-Chalcedonian forms of Christianity flourished in the region under the support of the ruling Sassanian dynasty. With important intellectual centres in Edessa and Nisibis, Persian Christianity developed its own distinctive tradition of thought under the influence of theologians like Theodore of Mopsuestia (*c.*350–428) and Nestorius (mid-4th to mid-5th centuries). Nestorian Christianity spread further east along the busy trade routes that connected the Roman and Persian empires with Asia. By the 6th century small Christian communities had been established as far east as India and China. But the Eastern extension of Christianity was inhibited by the existence of entrenched Confucian, Hindu, and Buddhist cultures that pre-dated Christianity and resisted its incursions. Without political backing Christianity was unable to do more than win over small, marginal social groups when other religions dominated a territory.

After the 7th century, Christian expansion was also inhibited by the growing power of Islam, a new religion which spread rapidly in the years after the death of the prophet Muhammad in 632. Though it drew on elements of both Jewish and Christian faiths, this new rigorously monotheistic faith proved far more successful in converting the Arabic-speaking peoples of the Middle East, and quickly won converts in North Africa and the Near East as well (the Persian Empire was conquered in the mid-7th century). Christianity had appealed mainly to urban classes, and had kept intact the Roman economic system based on slavery. Islam also appealed to rural people, and promised a more thoroughgoing reconstruction of society. By bringing together military, political, and religious power in a compact alliance, Islam brought to an end dreams of a Christian world empire.

Hemmed in by Islam on several sides, the Eastern Orthodox Church was nevertheless able to spread into Romania and the Slavic lands of Bulgaria, Serbia, and Russia, all of which came under its spiritual control after the 9th century. In the vast territories of Russia, the Church spread by two main means. First, through the success of monasticism as a self-propelled movement able to expand into non-Christian territory and establish bridgeheads of further expansion. Second, by the strategy of entering into alliance with imperial rulers, including the dynasty based in Moscow which became central to the construction of Russian identity and unity. The Byzantine model of 'Caesero-papism', of Emperor working closely with Patriarch and Church, proved adaptable to this new context. When the Byzantine Empire

9. **The heartlands of Eastern Orthodoxy**

fell to the Ottoman Turks in 1453, Russia was able to take over the mantle of Christian Empire, with Ivan II styling himself Tsar (Caesar, or Emperor) in 1472, and Russia gaining its own Patriarch in 1589. Some spoke of Moscow as the 'third Rome', even though the Patriarch of Constantinople retained considerable power, even after the Muslim Ottoman Empire took over Byzantium. Ironically, it was challenged less by the success of the Ottoman Empire than by its collapse in the 19th century and the subsequent expulsion of Greek Christians from Turkey. Though he retains the title of 'Ecumenical Patriarch' (patriarch of the inhabited world) and has an honorary primacy within Orthodoxy, the present-day Ecumenical Patriarch's diminished flock consists largely of Greeks in northern Greece, Crete, the USA, western Europe, Australia, and parts of Asia (Figure 9).

Western Christendom

The alliance of Church and Empire developed in a very different way in the West, and eventually the Catholic Church with its centre in Rome and the Orthodox Church with its centre in Byzantium parted company. The schism was mainly due to the fact that the eastern church was able to maintain alliance with the powerful Roman/Byzantine Empire, whereas the collapse of the Roman Empire in the West presented the Church there with different possibilities.

As imperial power drained away in the West after the 4th century, the Catholic Church had to adjust its strategy. With a base in Rome, widely distributed communities and effective infrastructure, growing wealth and lands, it had become an important power in its own right. In the former territories of the Empire, political power divided between competing warrior kings, princes, and prince-bishops. Successive bishops of Rome were quick to take advantage and to assume a position of unifying leadership in the West. They claimed increasing power for themselves, and started to be called 'Pope' ('papa', 'father') and to claim direct succession from Jesus' disciple Peter, who had been entrusted by Jesus with 'the keys of the kingdom of heaven' (Matthew 16:19). By the early middle ages no serious ruler in the West could afford to ignore the Pope. He had the power to legitimate those he approved and excommunicate those who defied him. Excommunication cut a ruler off from the Church, its sacraments, and salvation, and gave his people licence to disobey him.

Thus was born the idea of 'Christendom', of a unified Christian society under the ultimate control of Pope and church, and protected by secular leaders who respected the authority of Rome. By anointing the most powerful dynastic leaders in Europe, successive popes tried to establish a new line of Holy Roman Emperors in the West who would do their bidding—including the great Charlemagne (*c.*742–841). In practice, however, the ideal of an orderly hierarchy of power flowing from God to Christ to Pope to Holy Roman Emperor was continually disrupted as secular leaders struggled with the papacy for political ascendancy. The balance of power was such that neither side was ever dominant for long, and the struggle continued throughout the medieval period and beyond. Yet the Western Church did manage to establish its brand of Catholic Christianity throughout the West, and its unifying power was such that it brought into being much of the region we know as Europe today.

The means by which Christianity spread across the West and displaced indigenous or 'pagan' religions was generally top–down. When a non-Christian ruler was converted—sometimes from paganism, sometimes from an alternative form of Christianity like Arianism—he would be baptized along with his household and subjects. Gradually monasteries and churches would be established in his realm, often through the patronage of the ruler and wealthy landowners, and a more profound contact with Christianity might come about in the process. The progress of Christianity was marked by the appearance of stone-built monasteries, churches, and cathedrals, and by the end of the medieval period nearly every 'soul' was located within the parish of a local church and the diocese of a cathedral and its bishop— and often within the ambit of a wealthy monastery as well. Gradually the Christian worldview, its God and saints, leaders and institutions, established themselves as the 'truth' into which the people of Europe would be born and baptized.

Relations between Eastern and Western Churches were increasingly soured by serious theological and diplomatic disputes, and broke down completely in the 13th century when Western crusaders entered Constantinople. Greek-speaking Orthodoxy and Latin-speaking Catholicism remain separate Churches and religious cultures to this day.

Overseas expansion

The process whereby Christianity was carried overseas to become a truly global religion divides into two distinct phases. Both were bound up with Western imperialism. The first began in the 15th century and ended in the 18th, and was largely medieval in its assumptions and institutions. The second began as the first faded, ended in the mid-20th century, and was 'missionary' in a way the first was not. By the time they had ended, Christianity had established a presence in every country in the world.

The first phase of expansion was bound up with the growing power of Spain and Portugal, both of which began to extend their empires overseas in the 15th century. As they expanded into the Americas and parts of Asia like the Philippines, the Catholic Church played a central role. Religion and politics were inseparable: Spain and Portugal were both Christian powers; their monarchs were religious as well as political leaders; expansion was undertaken for gold, slaves, land, and souls; it was done in obedience to King, Pope, and God. This imperial drive involved the wholesale export of Western Christian culture and institutions. To be baptized was to accept the rule of the Spanish or Portuguese monarch and of Christ. The faith was spread by conquerors, friars (members of new religious orders), and priests. In this first phase of expansion there were no specially commissioned Christian evangelizers called 'missionaries'.

The second phase of Christian expansion was more modern than medieval. It was greatly influenced by the schism in the Western Church which took place in the early 16th century called the Protestant Reformation. This came about when those who wished to reform the Church were disappointed in their efforts, and brought into being new churches outside papal control. One effect was to give both Catholic and Protestant forms of Christianity a more 'confessional' hue, that is to say, they placed great emphasis on defining distinctive confessions of belief, often in written form—a process which was aided by the invention of the printing press. Another effect was to set Catholic and Protestant varieties of Christianity in competition with one another. In addition to this, a nationalization of religion took place as emerging nation states forged special partnerships with a particular church—whether Catholic or Protestant—which could help unify a territory and people. All these factors were important in the second phase of global expansion.

Instead of creating converts whose faith was a matter of external markers like baptism and church attendance, the second phase of mission sought a deeper and informed dedication of heart and mind. It could achieve this with the new, portable means it had at its disposal: printed Bibles, catechisms, confessions, hymnbooks, and printed pictures. Instead of relying on clergy and members of religious orders to carry out the work, this second phase of expansion created dedicated missionaries. The initial intention was that missionaries should be male clergy specially prepared for the task. In the event, a shortage of volunteers meant that lay people also had to be trained. Many were married men who wished to travel with their wives. By the later 19th century, women

10. Two missionaries from the Universities' Mission to Central Africa set out on a journey in Tanganyika, *c.*1902

were playing an increasingly important role in mission in their own right, even though they still had to work under the nominal control of a man. Given that women were denied other influential public roles at the time, missionary work proved attractive to many (Figure 10). Catholic women could join one of the new missionary orders, whilst Protestant women could be part of a missionary team. Many female and male missionaries became equipped with practical skills they could employ in the mission field, such as in education or medicine—for in the second phase of mission the offer of the gospel often went hand in hand with the offer of some of the material benefits of Western civilization. This second phase of mission took place in looser alliance with political power. Association between a state and church was still important, and modern mission was closely associated with Western colonial expansion. But missionary work was a more purely religious affair in the second phase of Christian expansion, and there was usually some distance between a Western political regime and the missionaries who entered a country under its protection.

Post-colonial developments

Although it conferred some significant advantages on modern mission, the colonial context did not prove to be an unmitigated blessing for Christian expansion. The most lasting and thoroughgoing success was in 'Latin' America and the Philippines, where religio-political conquest in the first phase of Christian overseas expansion, followed by more modern forms of missionary activity in the second, resulted in extensive and intensive Christianization. The most notable failure was in areas where Christianity was not backed by colonial power, or where it was forced to compete with entrenched religious cultures, as in China, India, and much of the Middle East. In areas like sub-Saharan Africa, there was generally more success, although even here thoroughgoing conversion was often less common than selective appropriation of some of the material and spiritual goods the missionaries had to offer.

To some extent, alliance with imperial power hindered modern Christian mission. Whilst it was true that converts could win advantages by accepting the religion of the powerful, the risk was alienation from their own culture and people. Consequently, the withdrawal of Western colonial powers after the Second World War has led to greater opportunities for Christianity than before. In this post-colonial phase, Christianity has been more fully owned and adapted by people who were previously colonial subjects. Many parts of the southern hemisphere have witnessed the growth of new globally networked forms of Christianity, most notably the Pentecostal and Charismatic forms of Christianity discussed in later chapters. Since their rise has been contemporaneous with that of resurgent Islam, it is interesting to compare the two. Both have flourished in territories that were previously under Western colonial control. Both have a globalizing tendency. Both represent indigenous movements of modernization. To be part of recent Islamic or Charismatic upsurges is to be part of global movements with the resources and sense of universal, triumphant purpose that entails. Individuals' horizons and sense of identity are raised from the local or even the national to the global level by belonging to these religions, and power is enhanced accordingly. Through membership one can lay hold of many of the benefits of modernity—including education, technology, and affluence—but without having to Westernize. The best of both worlds.

Ironically, the post-colonial growth of Christianity coincides with serious decline of churches in the West, particularly in Europe. It is estimated that Charismatic and Pentecostal forms of Christianity now involve up to half a billion people, the vast majority of them located in the southern hemisphere. This means that for the first time there are probably more Christians in the southern hemisphere than in the northern (around one billion in each). Since numbers in the south are still growing fast, due to high population growth as well as conversion, whilst those in the north are shrinking, the numerical centre of gravity of Christianity is shifting. But wealth and resources are still tilted towards Western churches, and migration into the West, new forms of global communication and linkage, and missionary activity, blur any neat division between northern and southern forms of Christianity. For example, many US churches still export a great deal of wealth and manpower to churches in parts of Africa and Asia, and the life-long missionaries have been replaced by those who are temporary, who travel abroad—particularly from the USA—for short periods in order to evangelize and give other forms of practical assistance. There is also the phenomenon of 'reverse mission', whereby countries that once sent missionaries become mission fields for Christians from former colonies.

For the Eastern churches, modernization brought much greater challenges. The modernizing Tsar Peter the Great who reigned between 1682 and 1725 abolished the office of Patriarch in Russia, and turned the church into a department of state. A reassertion of conservative interests in the 19th century went together with a revival of the church under the banner of 'Orthodoxy, autocracy and nationality', and led to massive reaction against both church and the ruling classes in the Bolshevik Revolution of 1917. Given Marx's attitude to religion and communist governments' attempts to establish control over the lives of their people, it is not surprising that churches under communism were often treated with ruthless hostility. In Russia, for example, the 46,000 churches of the pre-revolutionary era had been reduced to a few hundred by the late 1930s. But the state was also capable of changing its policy toward the Church when politically expedient, as Stalin did during the Second World War when he realized that the churches could be useful in motivating patriotism and colonizing areas brought under Soviet control. In Russia and Bulgaria, Orthodoxy lost some credibility as a result of its collaboration with the communist authorities, whereas in Romania, East Germany, and Poland, Protestant and Catholic Churches demonstrated a greater ability to mobilize opposition to the State, particularly in the 1980s as communism began to fail. Since then Eastern Orthodoxy has been attempting to re-establish power in ex-communist lands, often by way of active cooperation with new political regimes.

There has also been contraction rather than expansion amongst the Nestorian and non-Chalcedonian Christian communities in the Middle East and elsewhere in the modern period. They too have suffered as a result of wider political developments, though their fate has been shaped more by the energies of Islam than communism. The growth of more militant forms of Islam, and the disruptions following on from the Arab uprisings of 2011 and since, threaten some of the remaining churches that still stand as a testament to ancient forms of Christianity that remained outside both Western and Eastern forms of Christian orthodoxy.

Conclusion

Over the course of two thousand years, Christianity has grown from being a tiny movement within a Jewish context to being the world's largest religion with a presence in every part of the world. Its growth has not been smooth and uniform. It was most successful when in alliance with political powers, and least successful where other religions were well established and it faced unfriendly political forces. It has suffered repeated setbacks and retreats, from that occasioned by the rise of Islam in the 7th century, to the decline it is currently suffering in many Western countries. At no time has Christianity acted as a unified force. From the very start it has been internally divided, and it remains so. If anything, that division has increased. The chapters which follow explain its main varieties.

Chapter 4
Church and biblical Christianity

Some of the historical divisions within Christianity, including that between the Western Catholic Church, the Eastern Orthodox Church, and (later) between the Roman Catholic Church and various Protestant Churches, have already been introduced. Within each of them there are many further sub-divisions—schisms within schisms. Within Protestantism, for example, there are innumerable different denominations, and even within a single church like the Roman Catholic Church there are many semi-autonomous institutions—like monasteries, voluntary organizations, and different religious orders.

Understanding this huge internal variety within Christianity is less important than understanding the religion's main fault-lines. Some of these can run right through a church, as well as between different churches. Different scholars have various schemes and typologies for analysing Christianity. The one used here is a modification of the scheme developed by Ernst Troeltsch (1865–1923), the pioneering sociologist of Christianity. In this modified version, three main types of Christianity are distinguished in terms of how they understand and embody authority and power, both human and divine, and how this plays out in their own structures and their stances towards wider society. This chapter considers two types, Church and biblical Christianity, and the next one looks at the mystical type of Christianity.

Church Christianity

'Church Christianity' is so-called because it is centred around the institution of the Church, whereas for 'biblical Christianity' the scriptures have the equivalent position of authority. Church Christianity embraces the Roman Catholic Church, the Eastern Orthodox Churches, and some of the larger and older Protestant churches like the Lutheran and Anglican Churches.

Church buildings

The buildings favoured by each type of Christianity give a good indication of its characteristic features, and the churches erected by Church Christianity tell us a great deal about its priorities. Church buildings are not distinctive to Church Christianity, but they first developed with it, and have a particular importance in its life.

First-century Christians probably met in outdoor spaces, in houses, and—for those who still practised the Jewish religion—in synagogues. As Christianity developed and an emerging orthodoxy started to assert itself, it appropriated a common Roman architectural form, the basilica. This was a simple rectangular building rather like a Greek temple, which was designed for public meetings.

The basilica has provided the basic design for Western churches ever since, with a central room running west–east, a main door in the west or south side, and an altar at the east. To this basic form were added embellishments like transepts—giving the building the ground plan of a cross—and bell towers (Figure 11). As Church Christianity grew more powerful, its churches grew larger and more elaborate. The largest, called cathedrals, served as the seat of a bishop and the focal point of the regional administrative unit, the diocese.

The Church in the East, being wealthier and more powerful than that in the West, developed large and impressive buildings more

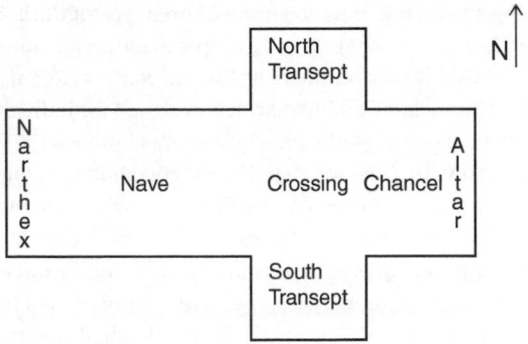

11. A plan of a church

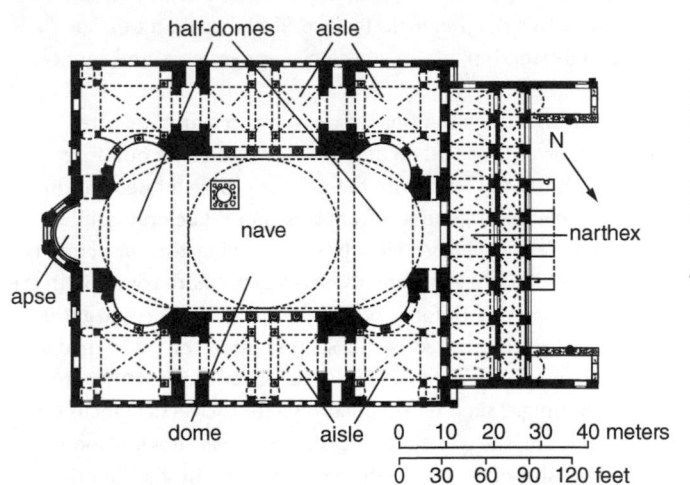

12. A plan of Hagia Sophia, Constantinople

quickly. The most important is was Hagia Sophia in Constantinople (Figure 12). As the latter shows, the typical form of Eastern churches is different from those in the West. They are often square or rounded rather than rectangular, with domes rather than towers. Both features which would later be taken over by Islam and become characteristic of mosques as well.

One thing a church tells us about the Church type of Christianity of which it is part is that gathering people together for communal worship of God is very central to its life—in contrast to, for example, Hindu and Buddhist shrines, designed for individuals to make personal offerings at their own behest. However, the form of churches shows that the worshipping congregation is not its main focus. If it was, churches could look like meeting rooms. Instead, they tend to be tall, imposing buildings with rich decoration. The interior space usually rises to the rafters, and from the outside the tower, steeple, or dome accentuates the impression of height. The effect is to draw attention away from individual and group towards that which is higher. This is reinforced by walls, windows, and ceilings decorated with heavenly images. The design carries a message: this religion looks to a world higher than this one. It demands worship, praise, obedience, repentance, and service.

As well as directing attention upwards, church architecture directs it towards a focal point at the east end of the building. The altar is located here, with the most magnificent decoration behind and above it, and it is from this spot that clergy conduct the ritual of the eucharist. Here bread and wine are consecrated (made sacred), either in front of a screen or—more common in the East and in the pre-Reformation West—behind it. People gather in front of the altar to receive the sacrament. A font, designed to contain water for baptism, may also be prominent somewhere in the building. Taken in combination with the vertical focus on transcendence, the effect is to suggest that even though God may dwell high above, He is available here on earth in the Church's sacraments. God made flesh. This sacramental focus is a key characteristic of Church Christianity. Though it reveres the Word, and its churches may have a prominent pulpit for preaching, the altar occupies the more prominent place.

The location of churches illustrates another feature of Church Christianity: its concern to maintain close links with political power and to influence the whole of society. Wherever possible, churches and cathedrals arc planted at the very heart of a village, town, or city. They are not set aside in some remote place as monasteries often are, and they nestle as close to the centre of civic power as possible. Cathedrals and abbeys are often found right next to the seat of political power in capital cities, in a way which vividly represents this variety of Christianity's desire to bring together God and humanity.

Church Christianity imagines power as something which flows down from heaven to earth. At the top of the pyramid is God the Father, in whom all power is concentrated. His power is mediated by His Son, Jesus Christ, through the Holy Spirit. The latter are the channels of power to God's designated representatives on earth, the clergy and political rulers. They rule over the people. The Church models its life on the heavenly hierarchy, and extends the model to the whole of society: the monarch is father of his people, the clergyman is father to his flock, and human fathers rule over their households. Thus a hierarchy of paternal order runs from heaven to earth, and the Church is responsible for the moral order of the whole of society. Church leaders and earthly rulers must work together to extend the Father's dominion.

'Catholic' Christianity

Church Christianity is marked by an abiding concern with unity. The Western Church calls itself the 'Catholic' ('universal') Church, Protestant churches of the Church type often claim the same title, and, as noted in the previous Chapter, the Eastern Patriarch is called 'Ecumenical' (*oikoumene* means 'the inhabited universe'). This concern extends to unity within the church itself, unity of Church, State, and society, and unity of the world. As the one true Church, instituted by the one true God, the Church type of Christianity believes it has a duty to bring universal truth to all.

This stress on unity was one of the reasons why this variety of Christianity proved so successful in displacing its rivals in the early centuries of Christian history. It was imbued with the same urge to expand and swallow up competitors that possesses many political and business empires, and it developed the inner unity and discipline which enabled it to do so effectively. The hierarchical ordering of the clergy—from pope, patriarch, or archbishop through bishops, priests, and deacons—ensured unity within its own ranks. The same hierarchy imposed itself geographically, with entire populations and territories brought under the oversight of dioceses led by a bishop and parishes led by a priest.

The authority of the clergy and unity of the Church are bound up with the sacraments. For Church Christianity, God is 'really' rather than just 'symbolically' present in the sacraments. The doctrines of 'real presence' and 'transubstantiation' hold that the bread and wine of the eucharist actually become the body and blood of Christ when they are consecrated by an ordained priest. The effect of this teaching is to elevate the sacraments to a very high position in Church Christianity. This elevates the clergy to a similarly high position, not because they possess any particular moral or spiritual gifts, but because they alone can consecrate and handle these holy mysteries. Such Christianity is deeply respectful of ritual and tradition. In an important sense, the Church is its own authority. That which is done by its leaders is considered highly authoritative, and the Church's own past—its 'tradition'—shapes the present. It is not impossible for Church Christianity to do radically new things, but the new is easier to accomplish if it can be justified in terms of the old.

One way in which such Christianity evolves is through theology, which until recently remained the preserve of a small number of specially trained monks or clergy. The high point of Church-type theology in the West came in the middle ages, when the project of formulating and imposing universal truth was expressed theologically in the movement called 'scholasticism', so-called because it had its origins in Christian 'schools'—the earliest universities—of the medieval period. Scholasticism attempted to organize all existing knowledge, Jewish, Greek, and Christian, into a single system which would provide a unified intellectual account of all things—God, man, the world, and knowledge itself. It proceeded by a distinctive method: asking a question, considering many different texts that had a bearing upon it, deliberating about their overall conclusion, and arriving at an answer—before proceeding to the next question. It was a highly skilled 'science' that could be undertaken by only the best-educated men of the time. The most important, for the Catholic Church, was Thomas Aquinas (c.1225–74) who wrote the massive *Summa Theologiae*. Thomas's project is sometimes referred to as 'scholastic humanism' because of the relatively positive view it took of human nature and human reason. Aquinas believed that 'nature must be perfected by grace' and was not fatally corrupted by sin. In later centuries Aquinas came to be treated as the official theologian of the Catholic Church, his ideas further systematized into 'Thomistic' manuals of unquestionable dogma. They were still being used to train clergy right up until the Second Vatican Council (1962–5), before the latter modernized many elements of the Catholic Church and called for a return to Aquinas's original writings.

The elevation of Thomistic thought was part of an attempt to guard unity in a post-Reformation Catholic Church which was spreading across the globe. Unity is hard to preserve and has to be constantly guarded. Deviation and 'heresy' need to be identified and destroyed, lest they threaten not just the Church but the whole social order. Church Christianity has always expended a great deal of energy in resisting external threats like 'the Turk'—the symbol of the steadily growing power of Islamic civilization—as well as enemies within. 'The Jews' were one group which proved particularly problematic, partly because many dwelt in Christian territories and were highly educated worshippers of the one true God who nevertheless rejected Christ and his Church. They were alternately tolerated, employed, admired, and viciously persecuted. Church Christianity (and some kinds of biblical Christianity) also devoted a great deal of energy to identifying, classifying, and rooting out 'heresy'—beliefs

13. Albi Cathedral, France (1277–1512)

and practices which claimed to be Christian but deviated from
the Church's official norms. Secular rulers often cooperated with
churches in attacking popular heretical movements with the sword
as well as with preaching and, by the time of the later middle ages,
by way of organized 'inquisitions'. The cathedral in Albi, southern
France, stands as a dominating reminder of the victory of the
medieval Catholic Church over the 'Albigensian' heretics of that
region (Figure 13).

Reformation churches

Given the Catholic Church's love of unity, the division brought
about by the Protestant Reformation of the 16th century was a

disaster. The aim of Martin Luther and his allies was to reform the Catholic Church, not to divide it. They were protesting about what they saw as abuses of its power, particularly by the Pope and other wealthy clerics and monasteries. What they sought was a purer, simpler form of Christianity closer to what they saw in the New Testament. They wanted the Bible to be accessible to all Christians, translated out of Latin into people's own languages, and put in their hands. But even though they eventually precipitated the most important split in Western Christianity, they always remained loyal to the main characteristics of Church Christianity, and the churches they ended up founding belong to this variety of Christianity—in contrast to some other Protestant churches deriving from the Reformation and discussed below which belong to the biblical type.

The Reformation was made possible by several different factors. One was a base in a 'Germany' which was not yet a nation but a grouping of independent German-speaking political units, some ruled by princes who were eager to take over the Catholic Church's wealth and power for themselves. Another was a base of support in the towns and cities, some of which were self-governing, and many of which were as impatient with the Catholic Church's privileges as the princes. Also important was the growth of a new class of artisans, manufacturers, and traders. As more people were freed from the land, they moved to the rapidly expanding towns and cities. Cities were harder to control than rural areas, ideas could spread more quickly, and some of the new bourgeoisie were receptive to criticisms of existing wealth and power. To this was added a charismatic leader, Martin Luther (1483–1546), a monk and theologian who could take advantage of the recently invented printing press to spread his ideas. Printing made it possible for many more people than before to read a variety of literature and join in theological disputes. Most important of all, it made the Bible much more widely accessible.

Luther read the Bible through the lens of the early Christian bishop and theologian Augustine (354–430). Whereas Aquinas emphasized the goodness of God's creation, which needs only to be perfected by grace, Luther, drawing on Augustine, emphasized its fallenness. He spoke of the power of God, the sinfulness of man, and humanity's desperate need of God's salvation through the unique work of Christ. Humans could be saved only through grace, and the Church was guilty of making it seem too easy to be saved—as if one could get to heaven by good works, not to mention by buying 'indulgences' whose profits went straight to Rome. The papacy's unwillingness to accede to any of Luther's demands set him on a collision course with the Church of which he had once been a loyal member. After his excommunication by Pope Leo X in 1521, Luther became the leader of a church which cut itself loose from papal control and distanced itself from what it regarded as its abuses and distortions. But despite its more biblical emphasis, and its more pessimistic view of human nature, the Lutheran Church retained the Church type's emphasis on the importance of clergy, sacraments, hierarchy, tradition, and unity.

John Calvin (1509–64) was a younger contemporary of Luther who saw himself as a faithful disciple and interpreter of the senior reformer. In his *Institutes* Calvin gave systematic theological and ethical expression to many of Luther's ideas, whilst also moving in new directions. For Luther the best a human being could hope for was to be justified in spite of sinfulness. Whilst agreeing that we are saved only by grace, Calvin places more emphasis on the importance of morality and law—not only as a reminder of sin, but as the basis of Godly life and society. He set about creating such a society in Geneva, a self-governing city whose leaders called upon him to help them experiment with creating a society organized by Christian principles and laws. From Luther derived the 'Lutheran' or 'Evangelical' Churches (as in Germany and Scandinavia), and from Calvin the 'Reformed' or 'Presbyterian' Churches (as in parts of Switzerland and Scotland). These were Protestant forms of Church Christianity, and in countries whose rulers embraced these churches, Roman Catholicism was displaced.

Box 7 Extracts from Luther and Calvin

The proper subject of theology is man guilty of sin and condemned, and God the Justifier and Savior of man the sinner. Whatsoever is asked or discussed in theology outside this subject is error and poison. (Luther, 'Works')

He is said to be justified in God's sight who is both reckoned righteous in God's judgement and has been accepted on account of his righteousness ... wherever there is sin, there also the wrath and vengeance of God show themselves. (Calvin, 'Institutes of the Christian Religion')

Like other forms of Church Christianity, Lutheran and Presbyterian Churches maintain a close relationship with political power, and try to shape societies according to Christian principles. They retain the sacraments (reduced to two, baptism and eucharist), and continue to insist on clerical authority, not least in interpreting God's Word. They also retain hierarchical paternalism, calling for total submission to God the Father and Jesus Christ, mirrored in a social order firmly founded on the rule of 'fathers'—prince, magistrate, clergyman, fathers of households, masters of workshops. By closing down nunneries and monasteries, and banning worship of Mary and the saints, the Reformation actually removed the most powerful female figures from Christianity.

Much of this made early Protestantism well suited to the needs of the emerging European nation-states of the period. By giving sole support to a single church in his territory, a ruler could use it to help create a unified nation and consolidate his power. New national churches like the Church of England, the Church of Scotland, the Church of Sweden—and many more—came into being as their rulers adapted Lutheranism and Calvinism, and broke free of the Catholic Church. Other countries, like France, made Roman

Catholicism their national religion. No matter whether a country became Catholic or Protestant, citizens who dissented from the official 'established' religion often suffered severe penalties.

Biblical Christianity

The Protestant Reformation's emphasis on the centrality of the Bible edged it closer to a second main type of church, the biblical type. Besides the 'magisterial reformers' Luther, Calvin, and Zwingli, there were other early reformers—sometimes called 'radical reformers'— and other Protestant churches which fall much more squarely into this second main type of Christianity. Some of the earliest are the family of 'Anabaptist' and Baptist Churches, Independent Churches, and Congregationalist Churches. Biblical Christianity only comes into existence at the time of the Reformation, largely because it was only then that the Bible became widely available in a printed form and in people's native languages. By modern times this type of Christianity would become highly successful, not least within the broad movements of fundamentalism and evangelicalism which are discussed in Chapter 6.

Biblical Christianity is centred on the conviction that life and belief should be in strict conformity to what is written in the Bible, not to any human authority. With the Bible as supreme authority, human beings need no priestly mediator with God, nor any sacramental channel. They can form communities of 'the saints' whose members are equal before God to the extent that they strive to live in strict conformity to His Word. This message could be democratic and egalitarian—since everyone could read the Bible for him- or herself—but in practice it was often qualified in certain ways, for example as endorsing male headship of women.

Whereas the Church type of Christianity casts its net over the whole of society in order to draw in every soul, and seeks alliance with temporal power to do so, biblical Christianity tends to shun 'the world'. After all, New Testament teaching, when taken seriously, calls for a lifestyle that is impossible to live out in normal society—including complete pacifism and common ownership. In this sense, biblical Christianity is inherently 'sectarian', that is to say, its communities set themselves apart from society and claim to be more faithful to God's Word than ordinary, 'worldly' Christians (including all who belong to the Church type of Christianity). Biblical Christians try to live as true disciples of Christ. They maintain a distance from the world in order to avoid being corrupted by it. Striking examples of such separation are provided today by the continued existence of radical Reformation-derived groups like the Mennonites and the Amish.

In contrast to the magnificence and the ornate decoration of many of Church Christianity's buildings, biblical Christianity prefers to keep things simple. It maintains that a true relationship with God depends not on such 'externals', but on a pure heart and mind where God is received 'in spirit and in truth'. This preference for plainness gave rise to iconoclastic destruction of church art and sculpture by some early Protestants. If they took over existing churches they would whitewash the murals and decapitate statues of Mary and the saints. When biblical Christians build their own churches, they often take the form of a chapel—a simple open space without adornment, and with pulpit rather than altar in pride of place. Protestants also introduced pews—necessary for sitting in a quiet and orderly fashion to listen to long sermons, rather than parading around more freely and taking part in rituals. Some ritual action, including the eucharist or 'communion', was retained, but was usually understood as a symbolic celebration rather than one which made God 'really' present in an object. Baptism retained great significance in biblical Christianity as the ritual whereby the believer—usually an adult rather than an infant—dies to the world and their 'natural', sinful life to be 'born again' as a child of God, set apart from the corrupt world. This emphasis on being born again has been carried into modern forms of biblical Christianity, even when they have abandoned strict separation from society.

Biblical Christianity is notoriously prone to schism. Once it is accepted that each individual has the right to interpret God's word for him- or herself, it becomes much harder to maintain unity. Splits are frequent, since anyone is free to decamp and set up their own church—on the grounds that the new one will be based on stricter conformity to God's Word than its parent body. This has often caused tension with wider societies and the governing authorities, and sometimes outright persecution. The latter was intensified in the post-Reformation era by the fact that rising national powers allied themselves either with Catholic or Protestant forms of Church Christianity. This meant that the unity of Church and State was threatened by the existence of alternative forms of Christianity. 'Schismatic' and 'dissenting' churches of all kinds had to be vigorously suppressed, and many biblical churches were forced into exile on the margins of Europe and, later, in North America. Yet biblical Christianity survived into the modern period and staged a revival in modern times.

Conclusion

In historical terms it is Church Christianity which has been the most successful of the religion's three main varieties. Both the Catholic Church and Eastern Orthodox Churches have been in continuous existence from the time of their embryonic emergence in the 2nd and 3rd centuries, and the Catholic Church remains the largest church in the world. By contrast, biblical Christianity is a more recent type of Christianity, with origins in the early modern period when the Bible first began to become widely accessible. Its sectarian nature and desire for shelter from wider society in order to retain Godly purity limited its growth. However, as Chapter 6 will show, a partial softening of its hard edge towards the world has made it increasingly successful in modern times. This softening has brought it much closer to the third main type of Christianity, the mystical.

Chapter 5
Monastic and mystical Christianity

Whereas Church Christianity locates authority in the church, and biblical Christianity locates it in scripture, the mystical type of Christianity locates it in the spiritual experience of each individual. It focuses not just on God the Father and Son, but more on the Spirit which lies beyond name and form. Its institutional forms are varied, and unlike the Church and biblical types, it considers religious institutions valuable only insofar as they help individuals find God. It is in the human heart that the divine is made known, not in sacraments or scriptures.

Like the Church type of Christianity, the mystical type appears at the very start of Christian history. In Paul's writings it is often hard to separate the two varieties. Some early forms of Christianity which were later condemned as heretical and gnostic fall into the mystical category, as do some of the 'Church fathers' whose writing was later accepted as orthodox. Because of its focus on the inner rather than the external, and on the Spirit's availability to all, the mystical type of Christianity can be threatening to Church and biblical Christianity. By the same token, it often acts as a fertilizing influence within the other types of Christianity, both of which have appropriated and institutionalized it at various points in their history.

The most important way in which Church Christianity has appropriated the mystical tendency has been in monasticism. Strictly speaking, monastic Christianity is not a type of Christianity at all, but a label for institutional arrangements within which men and women devote themselves wholly to the spiritual life. Monasticism has been extremely important in the development of both Roman Catholic and Eastern Orthodox forms of Christianity. Although biblical Christianity repudiated monasticism, it opened itself to the mystical tendency in other ways, including in radical Reformation churches, the Holiness movement, and—most successfully of all—in modern Pentecostal and Charismatic forms of Christianity which combine Word and Spirit.

Early Christian mysticism

Mysticism is not unique to Christianity, but Christianity supplied it with some distinctive ingredients. Jesus himself offers a mystical, internalized interpretation of Jewish religion, and there are mystical tendencies in the Jewish scriptures, as when God speaks about the 'new covenant' He will establish with Israel: 'I will put my law within them, and I will write it upon their hearts...and no longer shall each man teach his neighbour...for they shall all know me' (Jeremiah 31:33–4). Far from being bound by externals of religion, Jesus claims that the Law exists to serve humanity rather than the other way round, and has harsh words for those who use it to bind and condemn others. He criticizes the Jewish Temple and rituals, suggesting that his own life, and human life in general, is more important than religious institutions.

Paul also develops what some scholars have called a 'Christ-mysticism'. 'It is no longer I who live,' he says, 'but Christ who lives in me.' In his more radical moments, Paul says that all baptized Christians live in mystical union with the risen Christ. In his more cautious moods, however, he draws back from the egalitarian implications of such mysticism and the view that everyone can claim the mind of Christ by using images of hierarchy to limit its potential. Christ, he says, is the 'head' of the church which is his 'body', and some Christians stand in closer relation to the head than others. The Letter to the Ephesians, which was inspired by the Pauline tradition if not actually written by Paul, cautions: 'Wives, be subject to your husbands, as to the Lord. For the husband is the head of the wife as Christ is the head of the church.' Despite such precautions, however, Paul's theology was easily appropriated by mystical forms of Christianity, including the highly successful church of Marcion in the 2nd century which was later condemned by Church Christianity as heretical. As a consequence, it took some time for Paul's letters to be accepted into the official canon of New Testament scripture.

Mystical currents were present in Graeco-Roman as well as Jewish culture: in so-called 'mystery cults', in Persian and Far Eastern influences, and in the tradition of thought flowing from the philosopher Plato. The latter spoke of a higher and more real spiritual world and imagined the soul floating free of bodily limitations to inhabit a world of immaterial ideas. Some or all of these influences came together in the 1st and 2nd centuries to produce the many different sorts of religious, spiritual, and philosophical groups and teachings that were lumped together by their opponents as 'gnostic'. So relentless was Church Christianity's attack on them that for many centuries our knowledge of gnosticism came chiefly from the criticisms of orthodox writers like Irenaeus of Lyons (*c*.130–*c*.200) and Hippolytus (*c*.170–236). In older scholarship, gnosticism was often characterized in terms of its claim to possess a secret knowledge ('gnosis'), a dualistic outlook which opposed the material world to a higher spiritual one, a complicated cosmological myth of origins, belief in a divine redeemer figure who descends from the heavens, and a tendency towards renunciation of the world and the body. Now it is clearer that not all forms shared all these elements. The writings associated with Valentinian and Sethian forms of gnosticism, for example, develop detailed cosmologies, whilst other works, like the Gospel of Thomas, have no cosmological interest at all.

There was undoubtedly a similar variety in the nature of the communities which produced these scriptures. Some may have taken the form of organized and centralized 'churches' whilst others would have been more reminiscent of the schools of philosophy that were still common in the Graeco-Roman world. Rather than rallying around scriptures, rituals, or sacraments, members of such schools—often female as well as male—would be encouraged to think for themselves and debate with one another. In the Gospel of Thomas, for example, Jesus endorses the authority of women, rejects attempts to turn him into a figure of unique authority, instructs people that the truth is already within and around them, and encourages a view of the spiritual quest as an individual rather than group pursuit.

Early monasticism

As the Church type of Christianity developed, became more successful, and associated itself with the Roman Empire, it became less attractive to those who sought a less worldly spiritual life. One response was literally to walk out on mainstream society and enter an uninhabited, unsocialized place—the desert. We first hear of Christians journeying to the desert in significant numbers at the end of the 3rd century. Though they shared an ascetic desire to conquer the body and its passions in order to focus single-mindedly on the things of the Spirit, they were diverse in other ways. Some wished to live the spiritual life in isolation, whilst others joined growing communities of spiritual seekers. Both kinds helped lay the foundations of Christian monasticism.

We know about these early monastics from a number of sources, including a collection of 'The Sayings of the Desert Fathers'. These were men and women who ventured into the Egyptian desert. Though they lived in solitude they consulted with more experienced elders ('abbas', fathers), and shared wisdom. Their aim was ambitious: to attain the state of perfection that had been lost by Adam and Eve at the Fall and restored by Jesus. They sought to turn themselves into 'spiritual bodies' like Christ at his transfiguration and resurrection. In this state of perfection, the human spirit was believed to be united with God's Spirit, mind and senses calmed so that perception was sharp and clear, and the body in a state of such perfect equilibrium that it was able to survive with hardly any food or sleep.

> ## Box 8 Extracts from the 'Sayings of the Desert Fathers'
>
> The abbot Allois said, 'Unless a man shall say in his heart, "I alone and God are in this world," he shall not find quiet.' He said again, 'If a man willed it, in one day up till evening he might come to the measure of divinity.'
>
> There came to the abbot Joseph the abbot Lot, and said to him, 'Father, according to my strength I keep a modest rule of prayer and fasting and meditation and quiet, and according to my strength I purge my imagination: what more must I do?' The old man, rising, held up his hands against the sky, and his fingers became like ten torches of fire, and he said, 'If thou wilt, thou shalt be made wholly a flame.'

Instead of exalting the achievements of the lonely hero of the faith, however, the desert fathers continually teach the importance of love, humility, and a sense of humour. Only by humbling him- or herself can a person hope to approach the perfection of the God-man. Increasingly, however, we hear of men and women who sought to lay hold of divine power by extraordinary feats of endurance. In the Eastern deserts, particularly Syria, a number of ascetics became celebrities of their day. Some stood for so long with their arms outstretched that their limbs atrophied. Others exposed themselves to the heat of the sun until they were near the point of death. The most famous of all, Simeon Stylites (388–459), lived atop of a pillar for almost 40 years, giving counsel to the crowds of curious visitors who travelled to see him.

The asceticism of the desert also found more philosophical forms of expression. Intellectually, asceticism looked back to the work of the pioneering Christian theologian, Origen (185–254), who gave Christianity systematic expression by drawing on Platonic categories of thought. Origen told a cosmic myth of origins in which human beings are originally spiritual but 'fall' into their bodies. The Christian life is a struggle to rise above these bodies and their desires to return to one's spiritual origins. Such ideas influenced the most important theorists of early Christian monasticism, most notably Evagrius (345–399) and John Cassian (360–435). This tradition of asceticism pushed to the very margin of what Church Christianity in the West would tolerate as orthodox.

Box 9 Extract from Origen, De Principiis

Before the ages minds were all pure ... But the devil, who was one of them, since he possessed free-will, desired to resist God, and God drove him away. With him revolted all the other powers. Some sinned deeply and became demons, others less and became angels; others still less and became archangels ... But there remained some souls who had not sinned so greatly as to become demons, nor on the other hand so very lightly as to become angels. God therefore made the present world and bound the soul to the body as a punishment.

We also hear of more social or 'coenobitic' forms of monasticism, including that established by Pachomius (c.290–346). Members of these loose communities sheltered together for protection, not least from the bandits, criminals, vagabonds, and tax evaders who haunted the desert and sometimes posed as ascetics. An early church or oratory (place of prayer) might be built as the centre of one of these monastic complexes, with monks' cells scattered around. Some communities supported themselves by manufacturing goods that could be sold in nearby cities. This form of monasticism laid the foundation for much that would follow.

Not all early monastic communities were established in the desert. Following the model and inspiration of the schools of Hellenistic philosophy, some wealthy Christians also established monastic communities on their own land and under their control. Augustine of Hippo and Basil of Caesarea (329–379) are two of the best known. Both helped establish the view that social monasticism was preferable to more individualistic forms of asceticism, a view that would later be endorsed by Church Christianity, especially in the West.

Monasticism and orthodoxy

At first, mysticism and monasticism posed a threat to the developing tradition of Church Christianity. As well as criticizing the worldly tendencies of the Church, they aspired to divinize and perfect the human—an ideal that Church Christianity reserved for the God-man himself. The growing fame of the mystics threatened to divert attention from the Church based in Rome and Constantinople, and undermine its credibility. If the ascetics were seen as the new martyrs—witnessing to Christ through their suffering—they made an uncomfortable contrast with a church that was now in alliance with the very empire that had created the Christian martyrs in the first place.

The solution that gradually presented itself was for the Catholic Church to co-opt the monastic movement and bring it under its own control. One of the key moves was made by Athanasius of Alexandria, who harnessed the energy and prestige of monasticism for the Catholic Church. Part of the strategy was to ordain male ascetics and offer them places of responsibility within the Church.

Women ascetics were incorporated through the establishment of orders of female virgins under the control of bishops. Athanasius also wrote a highly influential *Life of Anthony*, a celebration of one of the most revered desert fathers, whom he depicted as a stalwart champion of the brand of anti-Arian orthodoxy upheld by Athanasius and ratified by the Council of Nicaea.

This takeover of asceticism by Church Christianity had profound consequences for both. As it came under ecclesiastical control, mystical Christianity lost some of its freedom and became more identified with the defence of orthodoxy than with experimentation in the spiritual life. In both West and East, the line dividing clergy from monks became increasingly blurred as higher clergy were drawn from monastic ranks—the origin of the continuing, though different, practices of clerical celibacy in the Catholic and Orthodox Churches. The Churches also began to model their liturgies on monastic practice. At the same time, monasticism adopted the scriptural, sacramental, and clerical tendencies of Church Christianity.

But the mystical impulse—and its more radical tendencies—did not disappear. In some circumstances monasticism was still able to retain considerable scope, especially in the East. Here, to a much greater extent than in the West, monasteries retained independence and were never organized into centralized religious 'orders' under the control of a single abbot, and sometimes under a bishop as well. What is more, the eremetical tradition—the tradition of the solitary hermit seeking wisdom in unmediated communion with God—continued to exercise more influence in East than West. In Eastern theology, where Augustine's pessimistic view of humankind had less purchase, the ideal of *theosis*, 'deification' or 'divinization', continued to be presented as the goal of the Christian life. Whereas the West tended to venerate saints only after they were dead and buried, in the East the tradition of the living mystic and holy man or woman continued unbroken.

> **Box 10 Extract from 'The Revelations of St Seraphim of Sarov' (1759–1833)**
>
> A dialogue between Seraphim and a seeker:
>
> 'I don't understand how one can be certain of being in the spirit of God. How should I be able to recognize for certain this manifestation in myself?' . . .
>
> 'My friend, we are both at this moment in the Spirit of God . . . Why won't you look at me?'
>
> 'I can't look at you . . . Your eyes shine like lightning; your face has become more dazzling than the sun, and it hurts my eyes to look at you.'
>
> 'Don't be afraid,' he said, 'at this very moment you've become as bright as I have. You also are present in the fullness of the Spirit of God; otherwise, you wouldn't be able to see me as you do see me.'

Even in the East, however, there was a tendency for the individualistic inclination of mysticism to be curbed and brought under the Church's control. The orthodox mystical theologians like Maximus the Confessor (580–662), Simeon the New Theologian (949–1022), and Gregory Palamas (1296–1359), refused to separate mysticism from full participation in the Church's liturgy and sacraments. They believed that the individual should not seek to be caught up in a mystical union of 'the alone with the Alone', but should seek God in the body of Christ made present in icons, sacraments, and the worshipping community of the Church. Thus Church and mystical types of Christianity became closely bound together.

Monastic development in the West

In the West monasticism flourished throughout the medieval period, and provided a home for a great deal of the mystical tendency in that region. Even though monasteries and religious orders retained considerable independence, their energies flowed into the wider Catholic Church, and the mystical impetus gave rise to many of its most important new movements and initiatives.

A key step in the development of Western monasticism was the widespread adoption of Benedict's *Rule* (*c.*547) as a charter for the organization of the monastic life. The rule gave unity to monasticism as it spread across Europe, and shaped it according to a common framework. It disciplines monks so thoroughly that it leaves much less room for the exercise of individual will and the development of a personal spirituality than earlier, less regulated forms of monasticism. Benedict envisaged the monastic life as one of silence, stability, renunciation of desire, and rigorous discipline. Most of a monk's time was taken up with the constant round of monastic offices—the eight worship services that punctuated the day—and the rest of the time with work. The theology of Augustine and the practice of Western monasticism went hand in hand. By suppressing his own corrupted will, the monk could be brought into conformity with the will of God mediated by the abbot, the monastery, the Rule, and the Church.

Box 11 Extract from the 'Rule of St Benedict'

In all things let all follow the Rule as their guide: and let no one diverge from it without good reason. Let no one in the monastery follow his own inclinations, and let no one boldly presume to dispute with the abbot...If anyone so presume, let him be subject to the discipline of the Rule. The abbot, for his part, should do everything in the fear of the Lord and in observance of the Rule; knowing he will surely have to give account to God for all his decisions.

The 11th and 12th centuries witnessed a new burst of enthusiasm for the monastic life. A reform of Benedictine monasticism in the 10th century was followed by the foundation of many new orders. Some, like the highly successful Cistercian order, sought a return to severe asceticism. Others, like the Carthusians, shared this ideal but revived aspects of the eremetical tradition. Women as well as men were caught up in the medieval enthusiasm for monasticism, often against the wishes of families, monasteries, and the church. It is in this period that the monastic complex achieved its characteristic architectural form in the West with a church at its heart, accommodation on its south side, and a cloister connecting its main parts (Figure 14).

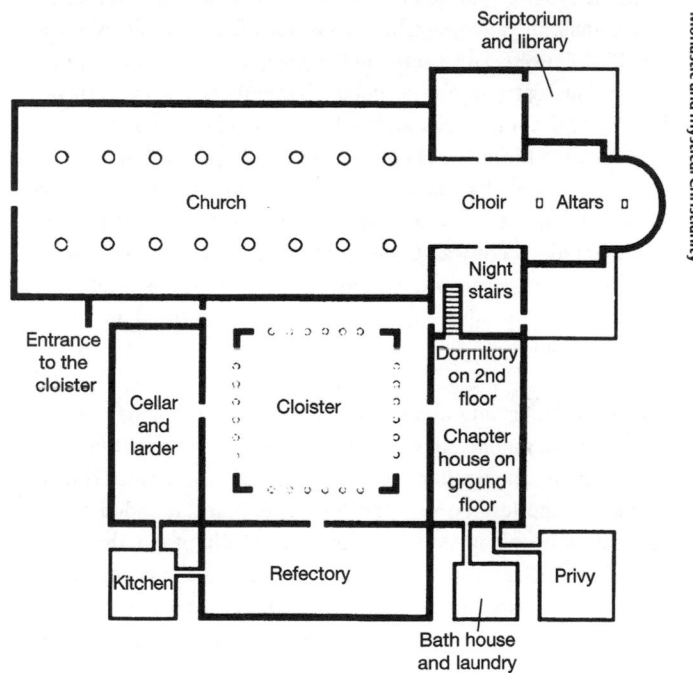

14. The ground plan of a monastery

Despite these reforms, the controlled, ordered, and cloistered life of the monastery proved unable to contain the spiritual energies of the medieval period. In the 13th century large numbers of devout Christian men and women sought an alternative context in which to live dedicated Christian lives. The very solidity and stability which had once commended monasticism now seemed to be weighing it down. The fact that the monastery cloistered itself from the world counted against it in the eyes of those who wished to take the gospel into the world. As towns and cities grew, and with them new and very visible human problems and juxtapositions of wealth and poverty, the monastery was becoming less relevant to Europe's most pressing social and spiritual needs.

Both the problem and the response were articulated in terms of a new ideal: the *via apostolica* (apostolic life). Its model was Jesus and his followers: constantly on the road, bearing no money or possessions, carrying the gospel to all members of society. Inspired by this ideal, some Christians took to the road on their own initiative—to the growing concern of the Church authorities. Since they had no formal authorization from Rome, a good number of these wandering ascetics—such as the Waldenses—ended up being branded heretical. Others were more careful to seek and win Rome's approval, and once again the Church was astute enough to see the advantages of taking a new spiritual initiative under its wing.

The most important outcome was the legitimation of new urban-based, mobile, mendicant (begging) orders, first the Augustinian canons, then the Franciscan and Dominican friars, and finally the Jesuit order (the 'Society of Jesus', founded by Ignatius of Loyola in 1540). As discussed in Chapter 3, the mendicant orders would later play a decisive role in evangelization not only in Europe but overseas. Though many women shared the apostolic impulse, their options were more limited, for it was not thought suitable for them to be independent, mobile, and mendicant, or to preach. They were left with three main options:

to remain within the home, to join a nunnery, or to enter into one of the growing number of semi-monastic communities which remained loyal to the Church but did not belong to a recognized order. Some of the latter were known as 'beguines', and were formally condemned by the Council of Vienna in 1311–13, but survived in parts of continental Europe for centuries after this.

Medieval mysticism

The mystical tradition inspired some of the greatest spiritual writings of the medieval period, and it brings us the first female voices recorded at any length in the Christian tradition. Some of the most prominent figures, like Hildegard of Bingen (1098–1179), belonged to women's religious orders and received their education within the convent. Others, like Julian of Norwich (*c.*1342–*c.*1416), were hermits, and still others like Mechtild of Magdeburg (*c.*1207–82) and Hadewijch (13th century) belonged to communities of lay women. A handful, like Teresa of Avila (1515–82), founded their own orders in the face of considerable opposition from the Church.

Whilst remaining loyal to the Catholic Church, particularly its sacramental emphasis, many women mystics sought a close, personal experience of the living God. They found it in various different ways: in intense experiences of communion with Jesus, in transports of delight, in experiences of inner abandonment and darkness, and in union with the divine. Some, like Mechtild, used the sacraments as a point of direct contact with Jesus and imagined themselves as brides receiving the heavenly bridegroom. Others, like Teresa, favoured a form of contemplation that moved beyond images altogether and in which the self merged with the divine in an experience that could not be described in words. It was also possible to use mystical experiences as the basis for profound theological exploration, as when Julian developed a trinitarian theology on the basis of the 'showings' that God vouchsafed to her. To this rich variety was added the work of male mystical writers, many of whom were in close contact with women mystics and their communities, sometimes as spiritual advisers and scribes. They include Meister Eckhart (1260–1328), Johannes Tauler (1300–61), Jan van Ruysbroeck (1293–1381), and Gerhard Groote (1340–84). They too existed on the fringes of the ecclesiastical establishment.

The medieval Church's attitude was ambivalent. It could hardly deny the biblical hope that 'your sons and daughters will prophesy, your old men will dream dreams and your young men will see visions', but it viewed claims to unmediated contact with God with great scepticism, and condemned any suggestion that the mystic could enter into union with God or dispense with clerical mediation. Some of Eckhart's propositions were condemned on these grounds, and the beguine Margeret Porete, author of the *Mirror of Simple Souls*, was burnt at the stake in 1310. Inquisitors were quick to accuse mystics of belonging to suspect movements of spiritual enthusiasm such as the Brethren of the Free Spirit. Before long, accusations of witchcraft were levelled at some women—and a few men—who were accused of using sacred things to further their own malevolent designs. In reality, however, there is little evidence that either mysticism or magic ever took shape in large-scale organized movements—other than in the imagination of the heresy-hunters.

Mysticism in early Protestantism

The mystical tendency was also evident in early Protestantism. In the 12th century Joachim of Fiore (*c.*1135–1202) had foretold an age of the Spirit in which *viri spirituales* (spiritual men) would inaugurate a new era of love, freedom, and peace. Such hopes had intensified in the centuries that followed, and some saw in Luther the fulfilment of Joachim's prophecy. They had reasonable grounds for doing so. Not only had the young Luther been influenced by the German mystical tradition, but his early protests against the Catholic Church seemed to indicate his desire to abolish a religion of externals in order to replace it with a more inward and spiritual form of Christianity. After all, it was Luther who argued that the inner conviction of grace in the heart of the believer was more important than external works, and Luther who announced the 'priesthood of all believers'.

Such hopes were dashed, however, when Luther and Calvin actually came to power. Far from leading the churches that took their name in a mystical direction, they retained the defining features of Church Christianity. Even Zwingli (1484–1531), the early Reformer who had seemed to go far in the direction of a fully spiritual Christianity, pulled back from the full implications of his position. Supporters of the Reformation who had hoped for a different outcome were forced to create their own, more radical, forms of Protestantism. Some of these conformed to the biblical type of Christianity, whilst others located authority in the Spirit rather than the Word and conformed to the mystical type. Of the latter, the most notorious were those experiments that tried to bring about dramatic social change here and now—often in the 'apocalyptic' expectation that this would precipitate God's rule on earth. Thomas Müntzer (c.1489–1525) became a leader of the German peasants' rebellion of 1525, and the town of Münster became a centre of apocalyptic expectation and social experimentation. Both initiatives were crushed by the combined forces of Church and State, with both Catholic and Protestant Church Christianity united in their violent opposition to what had occurred.

Though 'Müntzer and Münster' became shorthand for the dangers inherent in mystical Christianity, apocalyptic activism was the exception rather than the norm. The mystical tendency in Protestantism gave rise to many different versions of Christian community, few of which engaged in direct political action, but some of which constituted at least an implicit threat to the existing forms of religious and political power. Luther's disillusioned colleague Karlstadt (c.1480–1541), for example, rejected the Church type of Protestantism in favour of voluntary, egalitarian groups of lay people led by spiritually enlightened souls elected by the whole congregation. Others, like Kaspar von Schwenkfeld (1489–1561) and Sebastian Franck (*c*.1499–*c*.1542), had no interest in establishing new churches as they thought that spiritual seekers should form their own small groups for mutual edification and support. The latter idea helped inspire Pietism, a reforming movement within the Lutheran churches which became widely influential in Prussia in the late 17th and early 18th centuries, and whose political quietism and charitable activism eventually won it State support. Pietism, in turn, had a direct influence on John Wesley (1703–91) and his brother Charles (1707–88). The Wesleys were the founders of Methodism, a reform movement in the Church of England which eventually became independent, and which combined Church, biblical and mystical elements.

In the late 18th and early 19th centuries, a new style of poetic mysticism fused Christian and Romantic impulses. Its most celebrated writers are the English poet and visionary William Blake (1757–1827) and the Transcendentalists in America. One of its distinguishing features is its sense that God is found within the deepest human desires, longings, and sensual experiences rather than in renunciation. It was usually regarded as having placed itself beyond the bounds of orthodoxy and the church.

> ### Box 12 William Blake, 'The Garden of Love', from *Songs of Experience*
>
> I went to the Garden of Love,
> And saw what I never had seen;
> A Chapel was built in the midst,
> Where I used to play on the green.
> And the gates of this Chapel were shut,
> And 'Thou shalt not' writ over the door;

> So I turned to the Garden of Love,
> That so many sweet flowers bore.
> And I saw it was filled with graves,
> And tombstones where flowers should be;
> And Priests in black gowns were walking their rounds,
> And binding with briars my joys & desires.

One of the few mystical groups which succeeded in founding an independent, unified, and influential religious institution which exists to this day was the Society of Friends, or 'Quakers'. Its English founder, George Fox (1624–91), rejected existing forms of Christianity in his quest for a pure, inward, spiritual religion based on direct experience of Christ in the heart of the individual. Fox spoke of the light of Christ that illuminates each individual directly, and believed that those who know the indwelling presence of Christ have no need of external channels of grace. He therefore removed all sacraments, ritual, liturgy, priests, and scriptures from worship. Friends gather not in 'churches' but in 'Meeting Houses', and in worship they sit together in silence unless and until someone is moved by the Spirit to speak. Quakerism survived by combining a pure and formless mysticism with some biblical and Christological elements, a simple and sustainable organizational form, and a radical social conscience.

Conclusion

The mystical tendency in Christianity is as old as the religion itself, and its inspiration can be traced back to Jesus and Paul. This is the most disorganized and unruly type of Christianity, for it does not recognize the overriding authority of church or Bible. Rather than form its own enduring organizational forms, it tends to shelter within the ambit of other forms of Christian institution, to give rise to small loosely organized communities, and to inspire solitary spiritual pilgrims. Even though it is characteristic of mystical Christianity to insist on the radical implications of Christianity's boundary-crossing between human and divine, it can be very threatening to Church and biblical types of Christianity when it does so, and they are likely to insist that the marrying of human and divine is unique to Christ alone. Yet the mystical type continues to be a quiet power at the heart of Christianity, breaking through existing forms and inspiring new ones—as in the Charismatic upsurge discussed in the next chapter.

Chapter 6
Christianity in the modern world

Contrary to the view that Christianity is undermined by modernity, the period from the late 18th to the 21st centuries has witnessed its growth and extension to become the world's largest religion. Even though it suffered in the 20th century at the hands of communist regimes, it also benefited in the 19th and 20th centuries from being the majority religion of two modern superpowers, first Great Britain, then the United States of America. And as Western imperialism waned in the course of the 20th century, Christianity entered a new phase of revival and growth in Latin America, Africa, and parts of Asia, shifting its numerical centre of gravity south.

During the modern period Christianity has also changed in rapid and unprecedented ways. The main types of Church, biblical, and mystical Christianity can still be discerned, but they come together in new combinations. The most important take shape not in new churches and denominations, but in movements which flow through them and shape their agendas—most importantly Christian Liberalism, Evangelicalism, and Fundamentalism, Pentecostalism, and Charismatic revival. The growing interconnectedness of the modern world means that these movements now operate and compete on a global scale. Rather than being shaped chiefly by local or national contexts or an ecclesiastical centre like Rome, Christians now come under the influence of many different free-flowing cultural and religious currents, to an increased number of which they have unprecedented access.

In the later 20th and the early 21st centuries this led to a crisis of traditional authority in the churches which was particularly felt in those of the Church type. Increased affluence, choice, mobility, education, and access to knowledge undermined the authority of rooted tradition, local community, clerical hierarchy, and the parish and diocesan structure. Both biblical and mystical forms of Christianity have adapted better, the former by offering the Bible as a portable resource available to everyone, the latter by catering to the modern desire for personal experience, and both by allowing greater lay participation and embracing new forms, institutions, and movements not tied to territory. The combination of biblical and mystical elements in the upsurge of Charismatic Evangelicalism after the 1970s has proved especially successful in many parts of the world not dominated by competing world religions or hostile political powers.

Outside of communist countries, the greatest Christian decline has occurred in Western Europe, the traditional heartland of Church Christianity. In the 1970s, about 60 per cent of Christians lived in Europe and North America. Now it is estimated that only about a third do. Here, as in Australasia, Christianity now finds itself in competition not only with other religions, but with secular alternatives. The Western churches' decline began in the late 19th century, but accelerated after the 1970s. In the current population, each generation is more likely than the one before to identify as non-religious, with Christian cultural dominance being threatened as a result.

More than modern science, it is modern liberal values and a turn to subjective experience which have challenged and divided Christians. A first phase of liberalism in the 19th and 20th centuries, which called for human dignity and freedom to be extended to all men irrespective of class or race, was absorbed and often championed by the churches. But a second, more recent, phase of liberalism dating from the 1970s and 1980s which calls for the full extension of these rights to women, children, and gay people, and which shifts authority from external authorities to personal experience and choice, is proving much harder for most forms of Church and biblical Christianity to accept, let alone champion.

Christianity and revolution

The story of modern Christianity begins in the early modern period between the Reformation of the 16th century and the political revolutions which started in the late 18th century. The distinctive mark of this period was the rise of expansive nation-states in the West. As we have seen, the construction of national unity was greatly assisted by political alliance with a single church—Catholic in some European countries, Protestant in others. This alliance between church and state was undergirded by a shared worldview: power was the proper possession of a monarch—God in the heavens, the king on earth—who possessed the right and the duty to command his people. This was fine until the legitimacy of monarchical power came to be questioned; then the legitimacy of the churches came under scrutiny as well.

The most dramatic example came with the French Revolution of 1789, a rebellion against the monarchy which inevitably involved rebellion against the Catholic Church with which it was allied. The Revolution took place under the banner of 'liberté, egalité, fraternité' (freedom, equality, brotherhood), and monarchy was challenged by aspirations towards democracy. The belief that power was the God-given privilege of the few was attacked by those who held that it was the natural possession of all—or at least of all property-owning males. Some revolutionaries drew the natural conclusion that the overthrow of tyranny must include the overthrow of the Church. In the event, a more moderate and pragmatic policy of 'secularization' was pursued in France, which aimed not to abolish the Church but to bring it under greater public control.

This reaction against Christianity was intellectual as well as political. Criticism of the churches had been growing for a long time. Some of the earliest 'liberal' criticisms came from Church Christians themselves, like the theologian Erasmus (1466–1536) who had called for radical reform in the early years of the Reformation. Some biblical Christians attacked the alliance of state and church, and founded alternative kinds of church. Christians of a mystical bent could be equally critical, and the 17th century also witnessed the rise of early forms of Rationalism, some of which retained a Christian commitment. Thus some of the so-called 'Deists' in Europe and America retained a stripped down, rational-ethical version of the faith, whilst articulating philosophical and moral objections to the churches. In the wake of the violent upheavals of the English Civil War, and other wars of religion allied with emerging nationalism in Europe in the post-Reformation period, Deists proposed a new form of rational religion which would unite rather than divide. This 'natural religion' would be based on reason rather than superstition, would unite all men as brothers of the one God, and would benefit people rather than priests. By the 18th century, Deist and broader Rationalist currents were gathering force in Europe, especially France, some culminating in out-and-out atheism. Though it was still dangerous to voice the latter explicitly, philosophers like Voltaire (1694–1778) came close to developing what amounted to fully secular forms of Rationalism.

In France, the Roman Catholic Church responded with vigour. It condemned the French Revolution and the ideals that inspired it, including the desire for freedom and the aspiration towards democracy. It reasserted its monarchical ideals, and continued in its work of centralizing the Church and extending its control over personal life and, where possible, political life as well. It condemned new currents of thought, and encouraged the production of the Thomistic manuals of confessional Catholic theology mentioned before. As the first liberal revolution unfolded, the papacy defended its position as an important power-broker in Europe, and opposed democracy and liberalism. As late as 1864 the Catholic Church issued a condemnation of the errors of modern reason, progress, and democracy known as the 'Syllabus of Errors', and in 1870 it propounded the Doctrine of Papal Infallibility. In the process, 19th- and early 20th century Roman Catholicism became more closely identified with the forces of reaction and social conservatism than of democracy and social change. 'Fortress Catholicism', as this mode came to be called, defined itself by resistance to liberal modernity.

Not all Christian churches reacted against revolutionary and democratic upheavals in the same way as the Roman Catholic

Box 13 Extracts from the Syllabus of Errors (1864)

Errors condemned by the Pope:

15. Every man is free to embrace and profess that religion which, guided by the light of reason, he shall consider true ...

24. The church has not the power of using force, nor has she any temporal power, direct or indirect ...

44. The civil authority may interfere in matters relating to religion, morality and spiritual government ...

77. In the present day it is no longer expedient that the Catholic religion should be held as the only religion of the State, to the exclusion of all other forms of worship ...

80. The Roman Pontiff can, and ought to, reconcile himself, and come to terms with progress, liberalism and modern civilisation.

Church. In 1776, a few years before the French overthrew the monarchy, another revolution had taken place—against British colonial rule in North America. There were close links between the American and French revolutions, and many shared ideals. But whereas the revolution in France put Christianity on the defensive, the outcome in America was very different. Britain, which had broken with Rome at the Reformation, had exported its 'Anglican' state church to America (where it is called Episcopalian), but had also allowed other churches to establish themselves in American territory. Rather than ally themselves against the forces of revolution, as the Catholic Church had chosen to do, many supported the cause of independence, democracy, and freedom.

It would be an exaggeration to say that Christianity generated the democratic constitution of the United States. The men who laid the political foundations of the newly independent nation were mainly Deists who supported various forms of post-confessional rational religion. But there were many more traditional Christians in America who were supportive of the Revolution and its ideals, and who believed that good Christians could also be good Americans, loyal to its liberal ideals and constitution.

Most American churches had much to gain from a constitutional separation of church and state. Some already had direct experience of being a minority faith in Europe, and had fled to the USA to escape disadvantages that attended such 'non-conformity' with one of the state churches. Some of the churches in this category were Church type (Congregationalists, Presbyterians, Episcopalians), others biblical (Baptists), some mixed (Methodists), and some mystical (Quakers). Since there were so many competing churches in the USA, they did not want one of their number elevated to the position of an official church. So even though several churches in America had no historical preference for Church–State separation and religious toleration, they accommodated these ideals for pragmatic reasons. Before long their pragmatic preference was being justified in terms of theological commitment to religious freedom and toleration—resulting in stormy relations between the American Catholic Church and Rome throughout much of the modern period. In many ways biblical and mystical types of church were in a better ideological position to support democratic freedoms than the Church type, given their long history of opposition to political and religious hierarchy and their support for more democratic arrangements in their own institutions, but the Church type's longstanding desire to embrace wider society allowed it to accommodate constitutional democracy and religious freedom in the US context.

The upshot was that the rise of the secular nation-state and the gradual extension of democratic arrangements did less damage to Christianity in the USA than in much of Europe. Indeed, churches profited by being seen as integral to 'the American way'. We can see the results to this day in the fact that levels of churchgoing in the USA are about twice as high as those in Europe—although declining—and that religion continues to play a more central role in its culture and political life. Paradoxically, the formal separation of church and state has allowed each to support the other to a greater extent than in much of Europe where such separation has been slow and piecemeal (though today only a few formally 'established' churches remain, as in England, Denmark, and Greece).

Modern Christian movements

Despite these upheavals and revolutions, the modern period was one of enormous vitality for Christianity. In the imperial age this was particularly true for the Western churches, which by the early 20th century were seriously predicting the Christianization of the entire globe within a single generation. As well as witnessing rapid growth and spread, Christianity was energized by several new movements which cut across existing churches of the Church, biblical, and mystical types.

Liberal Christianity

The first and in many ways most successful of these modern movements was Liberal Christianity. This is the name given to the trajectory within many churches which supported modernity's revolutionary calls for more widespread human liberty and free enquiry. Christian liberalism was typically Protestant, but there were also unofficial liberal currents in the Catholic Church. Liberal Christianity was so influential throughout the 19th and into the 20th centuries that it seemed to many that it was bound to triumph over other less 'progressive' forms of the religion.

Liberals rejected the idea that the truth was located mainly in the Bible or in church traditions, and believed that human reason also had an essential part to play. After all, neither Bible nor tradition made any sense without interpretation, and why would God have given humans the ability to think for themselves if they were not meant to use it? Moreover, if God had made the world, there was nothing reason could discover about it which would undermine belief in its Creator, and nothing which science could discover that Christians should reject. As modern science grew in power and prestige, liberalism was therefore able to integrate it into Christianity. Liberal Christians often granted scientists sovereignty in their own sphere—investigating the natural world and its workings—but reserved to themselves the job of speaking about God and how human individuals and society should conduct themselves in relation to Him.

So Liberal Christianity had little difficulty in absorbing new scientific discoveries and theories which contradicted traditional interpretations of the Bible. The first and most challenging was the discovery that the Earth was far, far older than the 6,006 years that some theologians had calculated on the basis of the biblical record. The application of historical methods to the Bible also unsettled faith by placing question marks over settled beliefs—for example, that Moses had written the first five books of the Bible and that the gospels contained the authentic words of Jesus. Darwin's theories contradicted the account of creation in Genesis, and undermined the Christian view that God had created the world for the benefit of human beings. Moreover, Darwin's theory of evolution offered the first plausible account of how life might have come into being not as a result of God's design but through blind chance. Yet Liberal Theology assimilated all this by arguing that evolution was not an alternative to divine creation, but the method through which such creation took place. For liberals, accounts like that of creation in Genesis were 'myths' that contain deep spiritual truths but that should not be confused with scientific treatises.

Given its emphasis on human beings' ability to think for themselves, it is not surprising that Liberalism produced a great deal of theological reflection. The German theologian, Friedrich Schleiermacher (1768–1834), played a major role in setting the liberal agenda for modern theology, and in turning the tide against the more dogmatic forms of theology that had become characteristic of the post-Reformation period. Schleiermacher understood why his contemporaries were turning away from such forms of Christianity, but argued that they had misunderstood the true nature of *The Christian Faith* (the title of one of his most important books). Such faith, he argued, had more to do with a feeling of absolute dependence than with assent to credal propositions. In saying this, Schleiermacher grounded Liberal Christianity in the depth of human experience, even though he insisted that such experience is most fully and adequately interpreted in the light of the scriptures and the revelation in Jesus Christ.

With its emphasis on the value of human beings, human experience, and human freedom—including the freedom to think for yourself—Liberal Christianity took the first wave of liberalism in its stride. It saw itself as part of the onward march of modern history which would sweep aside tyranny and superstition, and replace them with more liberal political arrangements and more rational faith. This was part of its rationale for Christian missionary expansion and alliance with Western colonialism in order to spread 'civilization'.

Generally speaking, Liberal Christianity has remained a tendency of thought and religious commitment within the Church, biblical and mystical varieties of Christianity, rather than giving rise to distinctively liberal churches. With the exception of examples like the Unitarian and Universalist churches, it was most influential *within* existing denominations. This has sometimes led to conflict between those who accept liberalism and those who do not. Throughout the course of the 19th century, Liberal Christianity became increasingly mainstream in Western culture. It supported the interests and values of the growing middle classes and their politicians, whilst at the same time maintaining a social conscience by calling for amelioration of the conditions of the industrial working classes.

Right up to the 1970s it seemed reasonable to think that Liberal Christianity would continue to dominate the Christian, especially Protestant, world. Liberal theologians like Rudolph Bultmann (1884–1976) and Paul Tillich (1886–1965) helped set the intellectual agenda of Christianity, and in the USA the influential Civil Rights movement was led by the Baptist minister, Martin Luther King. By the 1960s even the Catholic Church was travelling in a more liberal direction in the wake of its Second Vatican Council (1962–5). The latter, convened by Pope John XXIII, brought to an end the 'fortress' mentality that had seen the Roman Catholic Church turn its back on modernity and retreat into a world of neo-Thomistic scholarship and obedience to Rome. The Council introduced a number of major changes to Catholic life and thought, including the use of vernacular languages instead of Latin for worship, the introduction of modern hymns and choruses, the liberalization of the religious life for monks and nuns, a more critical approach to biblical and theological studies, and an acceptance of the principles of religious freedom and toleration. The Council also ratified a new self-understanding in which the Church was identified with 'the whole people of God' rather than pope and clergy.

Despite the considerable success and extensive influence of Liberal Christianity, however, by the end of the 20th century it was clear that confidence in its inevitable triumph had been misplaced. In the Catholic Church the liberal direction of travel initiated by the Second Vatican Council was halted by successive popes. The process began in 1968 when Pope Paul VI, against the wishes of many Catholics, issued a document called *Humanae Vitae* which reaffirmed opposition to artificial means of contraception. Under the long papacy of John Paul II (Pope from 1978 to 2005) the conservative tendency strengthened, particularly with regard to personal morality. Although John Paul II championed human rights against communist oppression, he fiercely opposed changes associated with the second phase of liberalism including the legalization of abortion, the ordination of women, and the extension of equal rights to homosexual couples. The Catholic Church's failure to deal adequately with the abuse of children by priests reinforced the impression that it was deeply resistant to all aspects of second-wave liberalism.

Even though increasing numbers of Protestant churches, especially liberal ones, took the decision to ordain women in the course of the 20th century, they have also been generally reluctant to champion post-70s liberalism. Child abuse has not been a scandal in these churches, but they retrenched around a defence of the 'traditional' family (Figure 15) and the view that sex should be confined to heterosexual marriage. In practice this view often goes together with a paternalism which insists on the God-given difference between the sexes and, particularly in Evangelical and

15. *Family at Church*, by H. Fitzcook (1865)

Charismatic Christianity, the importance of male headship. Most churches have viewed a 'subjective turn' which has seen authority shift from external authorities to personal choice with deep suspicion. Even Protestant churches which appeared to be travelling in a liberal direction as late as the 1970s have proved unwilling to let go of clerical power or to resist the conservatism of groups within them actively campaigning against further liberalization, particularly in relation to the family and homosexuality. Overall, Christian voices which are anti-liberal on these issues have dominated the religion since the 1980s. Clerical leaders have proved much more conservative than their 'followers', and in many liberal democratic societies a gulf opened between clergy and laity which has widened in the 21st century, accelerating the process of secularization.

Evangelicalism

Like Liberal Christianity, Evangelicalism is a major cross-cutting movement of modern Christianity, though unlike the former it is confined to Protestantism. Although they grew to become rivals, Evangelicalism and Liberalism began with much in common and were often hard to distinguish—in the 19th century there were Evangelical Liberals as well as Liberal Evangelicals. But whereas Liberalism is tied most closely to Church and mystical types of Christianity, Evangelicalism has stronger links with the biblical type. By the end of the 19th century it had developed a distinct profile from Liberal Christianity, and in the 20th century they often defined themselves against one another.

Evangelicalism is characteristically concerned with clear statements of faith, and is therefore easy to define in terms of its own confessions. Most 20th and 21st century Evangelicals believe in the supreme authority of the Bible, the sinfulness of humanity, full and perfect salvation through Christ's atoning work on the Cross, and the necessity of giving one's life to Jesus and being 'born again' in a decisive conversion. In practical terms, Evangelicals uphold a biblical morality that affirms family values, and they tend to be active in evangelization and missionary work. Evangelicalism turns Christianity into an easily portable resource, a religion which individuals can carry with them throughout life, and which is not rooted in a particular community or locale. Every human being can read the Bible for him- or herself without the benefit of clergy or church, and their personal relationship with God is the very heart of their religion. Nevertheless, Evangelicalism rejects Liberalism's more sovereign view of individual freedom, for it believes that human beings must always be subject to God's Word, and that they are saved not by their own efforts but by God's grace.

For Evangelicals, the gulf which separates humanity from God is enormous: it can only be bridged by Christ. In this, they show their debt to Augustine, Luther, and Calvin. The most influential modern theologian to express this position was the Swiss Reformed (Calvinist) theologian Karl Barth (1886–1968). In his *Commentary on Romans*, Barth stressed the unbridgeable distance that separates God and man, and accused Liberals of cutting God down to human size by trying to capture Him in the categories of human understanding. In his multi-volume *Church Dogmatics*, Barth argued that humans can only understand God on the basis of God's own revelation in the Word—in Christ, scripture, and faithful preaching. Against Liberals who suggested that many people and many religions can contain truth, Barth argued that religion is a human construction that can never reach up to the living God. In order to 'let God be God' theologians must abandon their attempts to comprehend Him and have the humility to rely on God's Word alone.

But not all Evangelicals were as austere as Barth. Evangelicalism also had roots in more mystical and pietistic forms of Christianity which emphasized the importance of knowing God in a warm and heartfelt human encounter. For example, John Wesley, the founder of proto-Evangelical Methodism in the 18th century, had a conversion experience in which he felt his 'heart strangely warmed', and devoted the rest of his life to sharing this experience. His brother Charles wrote the hymns which gave deeply-felt expression to this form of Christianity. Many other versions of popular Evangelicalism developed in the 19th century and brought new life to Protestant churches, enhancing their appeal across social classes. Simplicity, lack of hierarchy, simple biblical teachings, and clear family-based morality all reinforced their attraction. By contrast, Liberal Christianity could appear more elite, intellectual, and upper class. In general, Liberals were interested in the Church and social reform, whereas Evangelicals were more bothered about individual salvation—but the distinction should not be pressed too far because Evangelicalism also promoted social reforms, including the abolition of slavery, and liberals often had deep personal piety.

Fundamentalism

In the course of the 20th century Liberal and Evangelical varieties of Christianity became increasingly divergent. This was exacerbated by the increasing challenges posed by modernity. A simple biblical faith was felt by many Evangelicals to be under increasing attack. Liberal willingness to support historical critical readings of the Bible, and their assimilation of Darwin, eventually provoked rebellion amongst some conservative Evangelical Protestants in the USA. In the 1910s, a small number united around the defence of what they believed to be the 'fundamentals' of Christianity, including the literal and inerrant truth of the Bible. They affirmed 'creationism'—the belief that God created the world exactly as described in Genesis. The result was a movement called 'Fundamentalism', a conservative form of Evangelicalism which made use of modern media in order to spread its plain and simple message—an approach inspired by mass media and advertising.

Although Fundamentalism was rubbished by many Liberals in early 20th century America, its supporters constructed a successful Christian sub-culture with its own churches, schools, colleges, shops, radio and television channels, and networks of association. It managed to hold its own against the influences of religious and social liberalism and to increase its numbers and start having an electoral influence from the 1960s. It re-emerged in confident and organized form in the late 1980s to make its voice clearly heard on the American political and religious scene, galvanized into action by a concern to defend 'biblical values', including traditional gender roles and male headship of the family, against the second wave of Liberalism (Figure 16).

16. Advertising God on a license plate, USA

Charismatic Christianity

Despite its effective public campaigning, Christian Fundamentalism remains a small movement within Christianity. Although they share a similar pedigree, Evangelicals have generally sought to distance themselves from Fundamentalists. Evangelicalism continued as a much larger and more influential stream of Christianity in the 20th century, and its growth was aided by popular, charismatic figures like Billy Graham, who were quick to utilize new media of broadcasting. But it is the third, and most recent, movement within Christianity which has grown fastest in the 20th and 21st centuries, often reshaping Evangelicalism in the process: the movement of Pentecostal and Charismatic Christianity.

Like Fundamentalism, Pentecostalism is a distinctively 20th century movement, dating from the same period. Unlike Fundamentalism, it started as a movement of the marginal, including non-whites and women, and it emerged in different parts of the world at much the same time. Its defining mark is the central place given to the Holy Spirit, and it is this which gives it its first name, 'pentecostal', from the story in the New Testament when the Holy Spirit is poured out on the disciples, and its alternative name, 'charismatic', from the Greek work 'charisma' used by Paul to describe the gifts of the Spirit.

The term 'pentecostal' is the one most often used to refer to churches which grew in the first half of the 20th century, mainly black churches emerging out of the USA—some being small, independent congregations, and some being much larger groups of churches which spread worldwide, like the Assemblies of God. Pentecostalism grows out of 18th and 19th century pietist and holiness traditions in Evangelicalism which stress how, through the gift of the Spirit, converted persons can be 'sanctified' and made perfect. As such, it has a more mystical and optimistic view of the possibilities of human nature—when possessed by God—than much traditional Protestantism with its more Calvinistic emphasis on the ineradicable stain of sin. Pentecostalism also tends to be more relaxed and informal about church order and institutions. It is fairly easy for individuals to establish new Pentecostal churches—anyone can claim the authority of the Spirit and set up a new church in a home, rented premises, or even the open air.

Because of its typically mystical view that authority is conferred primarily by the Spirit, Pentecostalism can be highly egalitarian. Those on the margins of mainstream society, even women and young people, can claim authority if they are believed to be genuinely Spirit-filled. Individuals who receive the Spirit are granted miraculous new powers—to speak in tongues, heal, prophesy, resist evil, and perform God's work. In the process, they often attain a new sense of self and significance. Individuals may feel empowered to take more responsibility for their own lives as well as those of others. Membership of Pentecostal churches can also bring benefits in terms of healing, childcare, economic assistance, and membership of global networks.

Although the terms 'pentecostal' and 'charismatic' overlap, the latter is more often used to refer to the second phase or 'revival' of Pentecostalism from the 1970s onwards. Despite this overlap, Pentecostal churches are often more critical of 'the world' and society, which they shun in favour of a strict biblical morality and the hope of redemption. Many Pentecostal churches have a strong eschatological emphasis, and look forward to the end of the world (the 'eschaton') when God will intervene and save His chosen and faithful people. Most Charismatic forms of Christianity share these beliefs, but tend to have a more this-worldly rather than other-worldly orientation. They appeal not just to the poor and marginalized but, increasingly, to aspiring and entrepreneurial middle-class people, and even to the very wealthy. Many Charismatic churches preach a 'prosperity gospel' which promises that God will bless those who are faithful to Him with both spiritual and worldly blessings, including health and wealth. They trade in miracles, and offer people hope of a better future not just after death but here and now. The entrepreneurial spirit of Charismatic Christianity encourages its followers across the world to aspire to better things—a resonant message for the late 20th century and since, as affluence has come within the reach of more and more people across the world. Such entrepreneurial drive fosters growth. The most successful pastors can become enormously wealthy, and some have established 'mega-churches', the largest of which accommodate tens of thousands of people (Figure 17).

Charismatic Christianity is the single most successful form of Christianity in the post-colonial period. It has flourished in alliance with Evangelical churches, to such an extent that it is often better called 'Charismatic-Evangelical'. Evangelicalism's traditional emphasis on the authority of the Bible has been leavened and supplemented by a Charismatic emphasis on the living presence of the Spirit. The greatest success of Pentecostal

17. Charismatic worship in a mega-church in Singapore

and Charismatic churches has been outside the West, in sub-Saharan Africa, Latin America, and parts of Asia. The movement has not produced a single global Church like the Roman Catholic Church, but is characterized by expanding global networks and different 'brands' of churches and congregations with complex and criss-crossing transnational connections. Compared to pre-modern forms of Christianity, Evangelicals and Charismatics set light to denominational differences and identify with any other Christians who call themselves 'born-again'. They emphasize the importance of the Spirit and of a personal relationship with Jesus, often irrespective of the particular church or network to which they belong. Since the 1970s, the influence of Charismatic Christianity has even been felt within the Roman Catholic Church—there are Pentecostal Catholics who submit to the power of the Holy Spirit, and Catholic churches in parts of the southern hemisphere which borrow from Pentecostalism to renew and enliven older and more formal styles of Catholic worship. It is estimated that around a quarter of all Christians are now Pentecostal-Charismatic—including those within the traditional churches.

21st century diversity

The 21st century opened on huge diversity within world Christianity. All three of the main types of Christianity were moving in new channels, and none were more threatened than those which clung to traditional forms of authority. The clergy no longer commanded the respect they had once enjoyed, theology had diminished in significance, traditional forms of monasticism were in decline, churches which allowed their congregations little scope for participation were losing numbers, the parochial (parish) system was in trouble, and church–state alliances had loosened. Yet many traditional churches, including the Roman Catholic and Eastern Orthodox, survived as great powers, and some of their leaders became world celebrities, even if their 'followers' failed to obey them. More recent

18. Young Catholics in the Philippines light prayer candles

movements within Christianity, particularly Charismatic and Pentecostal forms, thrived—particularly outside the West (Figure 18).

The old divisions in Christianity, between Catholic and Protestant, or Baptist and Presbyterian, had come to matter much less at the start of the new millennium than those between Christianity and other faiths, and between Christianity and secularism. Divisions within a single nation had also become less important than those between global movements within Christianity, which resolve themselves into five main kinds:

1. Conservative or Fundamentalist Christianity, which reduces the religion to a number of clear tenets, rejects liberalism in all its forms, insists that Christianity offers the only reliable guide to the natural world, humanity, and God, and mobilizes to defend what are seen as threatened institutions and ways of life (like the patriarchal household and masculine domination).

2. Other-worldly Pentecostalism, which turns away from the temptations of the world, gathers together those who have been born-again in the Spirit, and offers them the hope of a higher and better life, particularly in the world to come.

3. Evangelical-Charismatic Christianity, which has a this-worldly emphasis and offers immediate and tangible rewards and blessings—including prosperity and healing—to all who give their lives to Jesus and open themselves to the Spirit.

4. Liberal Christianity, which emphasizes the Fatherhood of God and the brotherhood of all human beings, and works to establish God's kingdom on earth—a kingdom in which justice reigns, the hungry are fed, the poor clothed, and the broken comforted.

5. Inclusive Christianity, which welcomes all spiritual seekers, has a strong mystical tendency, and affirms the dignity and equality of all individuals whatever their gender or sexuality.

Each of these different movements appeals to different social classes in a world which is increasingly divided between winners and losers in global capitalism. For example, other-worldly Pentecostalism attracts some of the poorest people, whereas this-worldly Evangelical-Charismatic Christianity appeals to aspiring middle classes. In terms of values, only the first is suspicious of all forms of modern liberalism, but only the last is unequivocally supportive of both its phases. The others accept the equality of all men and all races, but are hesitant about affirming equality for women and gay people. Some large churches, for example the Roman Catholic or Anglican, have within them followers influenced by all or most of these currents, many of whom find themselves at odds not only with one another but with their generally more illiberal leaders.

In the West, the institutional churches' reaction against the second wave of liberalism has been one factor in their decline. As each generation has become more liberal, so more have found themselves out of step with the kinds of Christianity on offer to them. Even so-called Liberal Christianity has often failed to embrace this liberal progression as fast as the Western societies in which it is situated. Outside the West, however, particularly in Africa and some parts of Asia, the churches' support of more traditional values and family structures has proved more popular. Indeed, the second phase of liberalism—especially support for homosexuality—is interpreted in some as a sign of the moral decadence of the West. Alliances between conservatives in the West and other parts of the world have strengthened the anti-liberal Christian voice worldwide, turning it into a major global force.

Conclusion

Christianity has not only flourished in the context of modernity, it has been integral to it. Many characteristic features of the Western world—its nation-states, empires, welfare systems, schools, and universities—are bound up with it. Modern values also grow from Christian stock, including the first phase of liberalism. But a second phase, which tries to extend equality and liberty to more groups, has proved a stumbling block to many church leaders since the 1980s. The late 20th and early 21st centuries have seen the ties between Christianity and the West loosening, and secularism and 'non-religion' growing, whilst the most vital and fast-growing forms of Christianity have flourished outside the West, taking the religion's agenda in many new directions.

Conclusion

In purely human terms, Christianity's achievement is remarkable. It has endured longer than the greatest empires and had more influence than the grandest cultural achievements. Its texts still shape lives, and many of its institutions still function.

A major reason for this success is the religion's variety and potential for adaptation. At its heart are a series of paradoxes: a God who is also man, a teacher who lays down no laws, a holy book which is many books, a monotheism which is trinitarian, a religion of peace which is often violent. These tensions provide inner dynamism. Christianity is a religion which seeks worldly power but worships a God-man crucified by such power; it fosters asceticism but preaches social justice; it views God the Father above as a Spirit within.

From this variety emerge the three main types and potentials of Christianity explored in this book: Church, mystical, and biblical. Each is an attempt to forge the truest version of Christianity out of the religion's reservoir of resources, and each burnishes one facet of the faith brighter than others. The confluences and divergences between these three types are one aspect of Christian history, their interrelations with varied social contexts the other.

Over the whole course of Christian history it is the Church type—which locates authority in church institutions, rituals, and clergy—which has had the greatest influence. From the beginning it has existed side by side, and sometimes in alliance, with a mystical type of Christianity, which sets less store by the externals of the religious life, and uses various means—including the monastic life—to cultivate a more inward and personal experience of God.

Both these types were supplemented in the 16th century by the biblical type of Christianity which locates authority primarily in the Word of God disclosed in scripture. It has grown steadily to become the most serious rival to the Church type. The simplicity and portability of a religion based around a text—rather than mediated by ancient traditions and a hierarchy of clergy—has proved attractive to modern sensibilities. As fertilized by elements of mystical Christianity to give rise to the global Evangelical-Charismatic upsurge of the late 20th and early 21st centuries it has proved even more successful. Today there are Charismatics around the world witnessing to the work of the Holy Spirit and constructing enormous churches and corporations. From the point of view of Church Christianity this seems shallow; from the Charismatic perspective it seems like a miracle.

The result is a contemporary world in which Christianity is as vibrant—and as deeply divided—as at any point in its history. Attempts to forge unity between its various parts have largely been abandoned, and its potential to act as a unified force in global affairs is correspondingly weak. Yet Christians sharing similar agendas are able to mobilize across national borders with a new speed and impact.

The wedge issue for Christians since the 1980s has been the second phase of liberalism with its demands to extend equal treatment and full human rights to women, children, and gay people, and its emphasis on the authority of each person's own experience, reason, and judgement. Whereas the direction of travel of the major churches up to this time was generally towards liberalism, nearly all have retrenched in the face of this challenge to traditional authorities, paternalism, and the nuclear family. Conservatives in the West have allied with Christians in post-colonial countries to resist change, and many liberals find themselves out of step with their own religious leaders. At the same time Christianity, like all the world religions, is experiencing a crisis of traditional leadership, and a growing demand for voice and choice on the part of ordinary believers—including groups who have historically been marginal to religious power. This new phase of popular participation, with unprecedented access to Christianity's rich range of resources, will doubtless give rise to new and unexpected developments in Christianity as it unfolds in its third millennium.

Chronology

	1483–1546	Martin Luther
	1493	Pope Alexander VI divides newly discovered lands in Central and South America between Spain and Portugal
	1509–64	John Calvin
	1521	Luther excommunicated; Protestant Christianity begins to take shape
	1534	Henry VIII takes control of the new 'Church of England'
	1545–63	Council of Trent
	1589	Russia becomes a Patriarchate
	1612	Foundation of the first Baptist church in England
	1620	Pilgrim Fathers set sail for America
	1647	George Fox organizes the Society of Friends
	1740	Conversion of John Wesley, founder of Methodism
Christianity	1768–1834	Friedrich Schleiermacher
	1815	Unitarianism organized in America
	1886–1968	Karl Barth
	1900s onwards	Development of Pentecostalism
	1910s	Fundamentalism emerges in the USA
	1911	Western missionary movement at its height
	1962–5	Second Vatican Council
	1968	Publication of *Humanae Vitae*
	1970s onwards	Growth of Charismatic Christianity
	1978–2005	John Paul II elected Pope, first Polish Pope
	1988	Election of first woman bishop in Church Christianity (Barbara Harrison, Episcopal Church)
	2000	Total number of Christian adherents reaches two billion worldwide, with equal numbers in northern and southern hemispheres
	2013	Election of Pope Francis, first Latin American Pope

Further reading

General Reading

Kirsteen Kim and Sebastian Kim, *Christianity as a World Religion* (London, 2008)
Diarmaid MacCulloch, *A History of Christianity: The First Three Thousand Years*. 5th edition (Oxford, 2010)
Linda Woodhead, *An Introduction to Christianity* (Cambridge, 2004)

Reference

F. L. Cross and E. A. Livingstone, *The Oxford Dictionary of the Christian Church*. 3rd edition (Oxford, 2005)
Adrian Hastings, Alistair Mason, and Hugh Pyper, *The Oxford Companion to Christian Thought* (Oxford, 2000)
Ernst Troeltsch, *The Social Teaching of the Christian Churches*, 2 vols. Many editions. First published 1912

Numbers

David Barrett, George Kurian, and Todd Johnson (eds), *World Christian Encyclopedia: A Comparative Study of Churches and Religions in the Modern World*. 2 vols (New York, 2001)
PewResearch: The Global Religious Landscape http://www.pewforum.org/2012/12/18/global-religious-landscape-exec/ (accessed 29 March 2014)

Chapter 1: Jesus: the God-man

The Historical Jesus

John Dominic Crossan, *Jesus: A Revolutionary Biography* (San Francisco, 2009)

E. P. Sanders, *The Historical Figure of Jesus* (London, 1995)

Images and Ideas of Jesus

Paula Friedrikson, *From Jesus to Christ: The Origins of the New Testament Images of Jesus*. 2nd edition (Yale, 2008)

Gerard O'Collins SJ, *Christology: A Biblical, Historical and Systematic Study of Jesus* (Oxford, 2009)

Paul

David Horrell, *An Introduction to the Study of Paul* (London, 2006)

E. P. Sanders, *Paul: A Very Short Introduction* (Oxford, 2001)

Earliest Christianity

Walter Bauer, *Orthodoxy and Heresy in Earliest Christianity* (Philadelphia, 1971)

Bart D. Ehrman, *Lost Christianities: The Battles for Scripture and the Faiths we Never Knew* (New York, 2003)

Martin Goodman, *Mission and Conversion: Proselytizing in the Religious History of the Roman Empire* (Oxford, 1996)

Chapter 2: Beliefs, rituals, and narratives

Images of Jesus

Gabriele Finaldi (ed.), *The Image of Christ* (Yale, 2000)

Jaroslav Pelikan, *The Illustrated Jesus Through the Centuries* (Yale, 1997)

Mary

Miri Rubin, *Mother of God. A History of the Virgin Mary* (London, 2009)

Christian Worship

James F. White, *Introduction to Christian Worship*. 3rd edition (Abingdon, 2008)

Cheslyn Jones, Geoffrey Wainwright, Edward Yarnold, and Paul Bradshaw (eds), *The Study of Liturgy* (London, 1992)

Christian Thought

Peter Brown, *Augustine of Hippo: A Biography*. 45th Anniversary edition (Berkeley, 2013)

Alistair McGrath, *Christian Theology: An Introduction*. 5th edition (Oxford, 2011)

Alistair McGrath, *The Christian Theology Reader*. 4th edition (Oxford, 2011)

Chapter 3: The spread of Christianity

Early Christianity

Martin Goodman, *Rome and Jerusalem: The Clash of Ancient Civilizations* (London, 2007)

Robin Lane Fox, *Christians and Pagans* (Harmondsworth, 2006)

Rodney Stark, *The Rise of Christianity* (San Francisco, 1997)

The Development of Christianity East and West

Peter Brown, *The Rise of Western Christendom: Triumph and Diversity AD 200–1000*. 3rd edition (Malden, 2012)

Judith Herrin, *Byzantium: The Surprising Life of a Medieval Empire* (Harmondsworth, 2008)

Judith Herrin, *The Formation of Christendom* (Princeton, 1989)

Medieval Christianity

Jacques Le Goff, *Medieval Civilization 400–1500* (Oxford, 1988)

Miri Rubin (ed.), *Medieval Christianity in Practice* (Princeton, 2009)

R. W. Southern, *Western Society and the Church in the Middle Ages* (Harmondsworth, 1990)

Protestant Reformation

Patrick Collinson, *The Reformation*. New edition (Phoenix, 2005)

Diarmaid MacCulloch, *Reformation: Europe's House Divided 1490–1700* (London, 2003)

Mission, Expansion, and Struggle

Mark Noll, *The Old Religion in a New World: The History of North American Christianity* (Grand Rapids, 2001)

Dana L. Robert, *Christian Mission: How Christianity Became a World Religion* (New York, 2009)

Stephen Runciman, *The Orthodox Churches and the Secular State* (London, 1971)

Brian Stanley, *The World Missionary Conference: Edinburgh 1910* (Grand Rapids, 2009)

Chapter 4: Church and biblical Christianity

Catholicism and Orthodoxy

John L. Allen, Jr, *The Catholic Church: What Everyone Needs to Know* (New York, 2014)

John Binns, *An Introduction to the Christian Orthodox Churches* (Cambridge, 2002)

Gerard O'Collins, *Catholicism: A Very Short Introduction* (Oxford, 2008)

John O'Malley, *A History of the Popes* (London, 2009)

Timothy Ware, *The Orthodox Church*. Revised edition (Harmondsworth, 1993)

Protestantism

Charlotte Methuen, *Luther and Calvin: Religious Revolutionaries* (London, 2011)

Mark Noll, *Protestantism: A Very Short Introduction* (Oxford, 2011)

George H. Williams, *The Radical Reformation*. 3rd edition (Philadelphia, 2013)

Fundamentalism and Evangelicalism

George Marsden, *Fundamentalism and American Culture* (New York, 2006)

Brian Stanley, *The Global Diffusion of Evangelicalism: The Age of Billy Graham and John Stott* (London, 2013)

Chapter 5: Monastic and mystical Christianity

Asceticism and Monasticism

Peter Brown, *The Body and Society: Men, Women and Sexual Renunciation in Early Christianity* (London, 1990)

C. H. Lawrence, *Medieval Monasticism: Forms of Religious Life in Western Europe in the Middle Ages* (London, 2000)

Benedicta Ward (ed.), *The Desert Fathers: Sayings of the Early Christian Monks* (Harmondsworth, 2003)

Mysticism

Olivier Clement, Jeremy Hummerstone, and Theodore Berkeley (eds), *The Roots of Christian Mysticism: Texts from the Patristic Era with Commentary* (New York, 2013)

Ben Pink Dandelion, *The Quakers: A Very Short Introduction* (Oxford 2008)

Amy Hollywood and Patricia Beckman (eds), *The Cambridge Companion to Christian Mysticism* (Cambridge, 2012)

Diarmaid MacCulloch, *Silence: A Christian History* (London, 2013)

Bernard McGinn, ed., *Texts of Christian Mysticism* (New York, 2006)

Chapter 6: Christianity in the modern world

Christianity East and West

Hugh McLeod, *Religion and the People of Western Europe 1789–1990* (Oxford, 1997)

Hugh McLeod, *The Religious Crisis of the 1960s* (Oxford, 2008)

Hugh McLeod and Werner Ustorf (eds), *The Decline of Christendom in Western Europe, 1750–2000* (Cambridge, 1999)

Robert Wuthnow, *The Restructuring of American Religion: Society and Faith since World War II* (Princeton, 1990)

Jane Ellis, *The Russian Orthodox Church: A Contemporary History* (London, 1986)

World Christianity

Noel Davies and Martin Conway (eds), *World Christianity in the 20th Century: Core Text* (London, 2008)

Noel Davies and Martin Conway (eds), *World Christianity in the 20th Century: A Reader* (London, 2008)

Philip Jenkins, *The Next Christendom: The Coming of Global Christianity*. 3rd edition (New York, 2012)

Evangelical and Charismatic Christianity

Allan Anderson, *An Introduction to Pentecostalism*. 2nd edition (Cambridge, 2013)

Allan Anderson, *To the Ends of the Earth: Pentecostalism and the Transformation of World Christianity* (New York, 2013)

David Martin, *Pentecostalism: The World their Parish* (Oxford, 2001)

Christian Thought

Rachel Muers and David Ford (eds), *The Modern Theologians: An Introduction to Christian Theology since 1918*. 3rd edition (Oxford, 1997)

Susan Parsons (ed.), *The Cambridge Companion to Feminist Theology* (Cambridge, 2002)

Index